Keynote

ELEMENTARY
Student's Book

David Bohlke
with Stephanie Parker

Contents

PRONUNCIATION	READING	LISTENING	SPEAKING	WRITING
Types of film and music Present simple endings	Traditional music for a new generation	My passion for music Listening skill: Listening for a reason	Talking about favourites Talking about likes and dislikes Communication skill: Showing interest	Introducing yourself by email
Weak forms (1): *of* and *to* Intonation in questions	Buy nothing new month	How I spend my money Listening skill: Listening for negatives	Talking about shopping Asking about shopping habits Communication skill: Adding extra information	Sharing information online
Word linking (1) /dju:/	A dancer's dream	A fun job Listening skill: Listening selectively	Talking about jobs Talking about a future job Communication skill: Asking for clarification	Describing a dream job
/ɪ/ and /i:/ *can* and *can't*	Pro gaming: a dream career?	A unique ability Listening skill: Recognizing unstressed words	Talking about abilities A talented class Communication skill: Conversation fillers	Describing an unusual ability
Sentence stress Sentence stress with modifiers	Flying like a bird	How I used drones to make an amazing video Listening skill: Listening for attitude	Talking about gadgets Wearable technology Communication skill: Responding to ideas	Writing an online review
/e/ Linking with /r/	Seeing with the mind	It's no big deal Listening skill: Listening for contrasts	Talking about challenges Dealing with exam stress Communication skill: Inviting opinions	Posting a challenge online

PRONUNCIATION	READING	LISTENING	SPEAKING	WRITING
Weak forms (2): The schwa /ə/ sound Stressed and weak syllables	Life in the Altiplano	An amazing place Listening skill: Listening for content words	Talking about places What do you know? Communication skill: Expressing agreement	Making a recommendation
Word stress Stress with modifying adverbs	The pressure to be 'perfect'	Like mother, like daughter Listening skill: Listening for similarities	Talking about family A film of your life Communication skill: Choosing not to answer a question	Describing a friend
Silent letters Regular past endings	From Pole to Pole	My great achievement Listening skill: Listening for past tense expressions	Talking about an achievement Round-the-world adventure Communication skill: Interrupting politely	Writing a biography
Combinations of consonants Positive intonation	Breathing new life into the old place	The place where I grew up Listening skill: Identifying pros and cons	What's your neighbourhood like? The right part of town Communication skill: Describing steps	Writing a proposal
Compound words Stress with opinions	When reality is stranger than fiction	My perfect photo Listening skill: Listening for opinions	What do you think? Is it real? Communication skill: Asking about spelling	Describing a photo
Word linking (2) Listening for unstressed words	Learning to use 'the most beautiful invention'	My healthy (and unhealthy) habits Listening skill: Recognizing linking sounds	Is that healthy? Healthy choices Communication skill: Disagreeing politely	Giving health tips

TED Talk transcripts 160

Featured TED Talks

Unit 1
Bluegrass virtuosity from ...
New Jersey?
Sleepy Man Banjo Boys

Unit 2
Wearing nothing new
Jessi Arrington

Unit 3
The joy of surfing in ice-cold water
Chris Burkard

Unit 4
The orchestra in my mouth
Tom Thum

Unit 5
Fly with the Jetman
Yves Rossy

Unit 6
How I use sonar to navigate the world
Daniel Kish

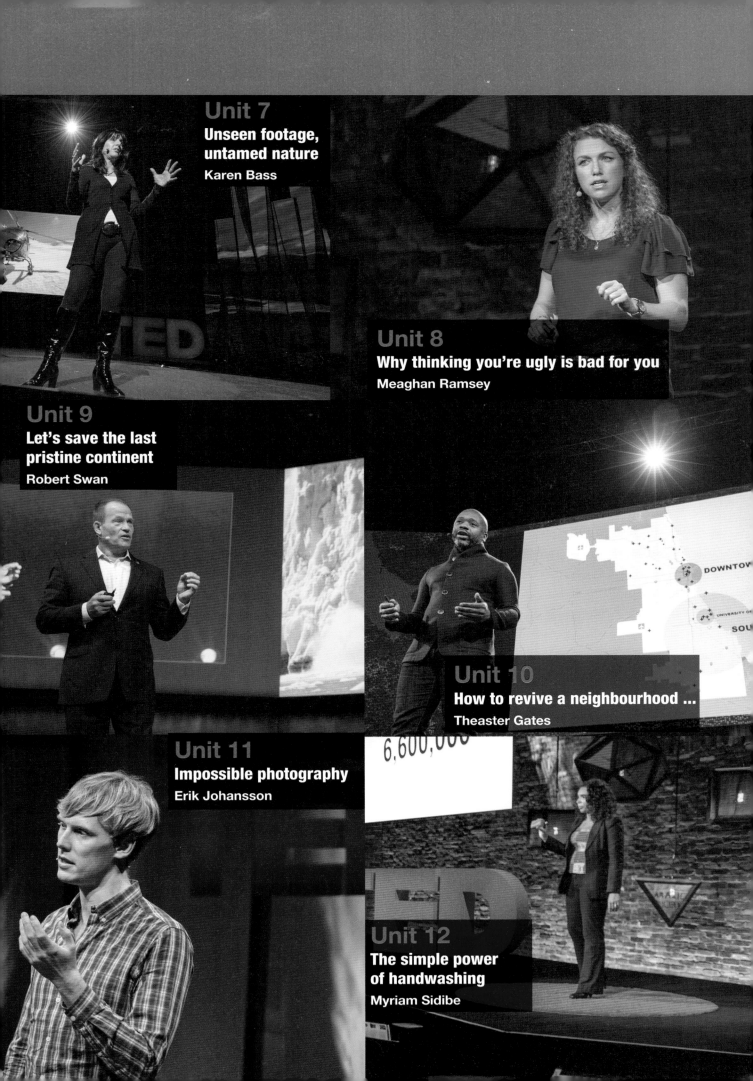

Unit 7
Unseen footage, untamed nature
Karen Bass

Unit 8
Why thinking you're ugly is bad for you
Meaghan Ramsey

Unit 9
Let's save the last pristine continent
Robert Swan

Unit 10
How to revive a neighbourhood ...
Theaster Gates

Unit 11
Impossible photography
Erik Johansson

Unit 12
The simple power of handwashing
Myriam Sidibe

What is **TED** ?

TED has a simple goal: to spread great ideas. Every year, hundreds of presenters share ideas at TED events around the world. Millions of people watch TED Talks online. The talks inspire many people to change their attitudes and their lives.

SPREADING IDEAS WORLDWIDE

Over **17,000**
TEDx events in more than
130 countries

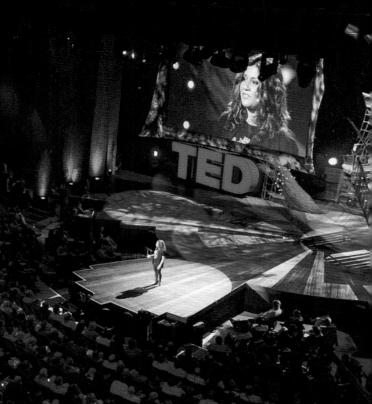

Over **2,300**
TEDTALKS available on TED.com

TEDTALKS
translated into
113 languages

Over
3,800,000,000
views of **TED**TALKS across all platforms

1 Passions

Ron Broomfield, from Lancashire, UK, collected about 2,000 gnomes and raised thousands of pounds for charity

WARM UP

Look at the photo and read the caption. Discuss the questions.

1 Why do you think Ron Broomfield started his collection?

2 What does the photo tell us about Ron's relationship with his gnomes?

3 Do you collect anything or have a passion for something?

In this unit you:

- talk about music and films
- discuss likes and interests
- watch a TED Talk by **SLEEPY MAN BANJO BOYS**

A musician plays the banjo outside his house

1.1 Do you like country music?

VOCABULARY Music and film

1 Complete the table using these types of music and film.

action	country	jazz	romantic comedy
classical	horror	rock	science fiction

Music	Film

2 Work in pairs. Can you add two more words to each column? Think of one example for each type of music and film.

Pronunciation Types of film and music

3 ▶ **1.1** Listen and repeat.

1 rock	**3** pop	**5** jazz	**7** horror	**9** science fiction
2 country	**4** folk	**6** classical	**8** action	**10** romantic comedy

LISTENING My passion for music

Listening for a reason
Before you listen, look carefully at the task. Ask yourself, 'What am I listening for?' Think about possible words you may hear.

4 ▶ **1.2** Listen to musician Philip Jones describing his passion. Tick (✓) the musical instruments he owns.

a bass guitar   **c** banjo   **e** acoustic guitar

b mandolin   **d** ukulele   **f** electric guitar

5 ▶ **1.2** Listen again. Circle the correct options.

  1 Philip Jones is from *England* / *Ireland*.

  2 He's a member of an Irish *rock* / *folk* band.

Philip Jones
performs live

SPEAKING Talking about favourites

6 Work in pairs. What types of music and film do you like?

> I like romantic comedies.
> How about you?

> I like action movies.

7 ▶ **1.3** Listen to the conversation. Do the two people like the same kind of music?

A: Oh, listen! This is my favourite piece of music!

B: Really? Who's the composer?

A: Bach. I **love his music.**   like his music a lot / really like his music

B: Yeah? I don't know him very well.

A: Oh, I think his music is **amazing.**   incredible / wonderful

B: Yeah? I don't like classical music **that much.**   so much / very much

A: Really? So what **kind of** music do you like?   sort of / type of

B: Anything really. My favourite singer is Bruno Mars.

8 Practise the conversation with a partner. Practise again using the words on the right.

9 Write one favourite for each category. Work in a group. Share your ideas.

  1 singer: _____   **3** actor: _____

  2 song: _____   **4** film: _____

> My favourite singer is Taylor Swift.

> Really? What's your favourite song?

1.2 What's your favourite?

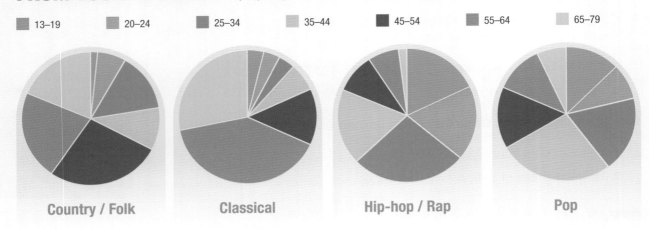

MUSIC POPULARITY FROM YOUNG TO OLD

The data shows the percentage spending on music by different age groups in the United Kingdom. For example, hip-hop/rap is most popular with people aged 25–34. Most people who like classical music are over 55.

- 13–19
- 20–24
- 25–34
- 35–44
- 45–54
- 55–64
- 65–79

Country / Folk   Classical   Hip-hop / Rap   Pop

GRAMMAR Present simple

1 ▶ **1.4** Look at the infographic. What is the favourite music for each age group?

2 ▶ **1.5** Listen to two people talking about the information. Circle the correct words.

1 The man's grandmother *likes / doesn't like* classical music.

2 She *likes / doesn't like* pop music.

3 The man *likes / doesn't like* rap music.

4 He *loves / hates* pop music.

3 Read the sentences in the Grammar box. Answer the questions (a–c).

PRESENT SIMPLE

What **does** it **show**?

It **shows** how popular different kinds of music are.

She **doesn't like** classical music at all.

a What word do you add in a question with *he/she/it*?

b What letter do you add to the verb with *he/she/it*?

c What words do you add to make *he/she/it* sentences negative?

Check your answers on page 137 and do Exercises 1–3.

Pronunciation Present simple endings

4a ▶ **1.6** Listen to how the ending of each verb is pronounced.

1 My father hate**s** rock music.

2 My teacher like**s** jazz.

3 She love**s** her job.

4 No, but my sister do**es**.

5 She only watch**es** comedy films.

4b ▶ **1.6** Listen again and add each verb to the correct column in the table.

/s/	/z/	/ɪz/
makes	plays	washes

5 Complete the sentences with the correct verb.

> don't like   is   listen to   loves   play   sings

1 My favourite book _____ *1984*.

2 I _____ the piano in a band.

3 I _____ romantic comedies.

4 My sister _____ really well.

5 My best friend _____ science fiction.

6 My parents _____ jazz music on the radio.

6 Change the sentences in Exercise 5 so they are true for you.

LANGUAGE FOCUS Talking about likes and interests

7 ▷ **1.7** Study the examples in the Language focus box.

TALKING ABOUT LIKES AND INTERESTS

What**'s** your favourite film?	My favourite film **is** *Titanic.*
Who **are** your favourite actors?	My favourite actors **are** Leonardo DiCaprio and Kate Winslet.
Do you **like** K-pop? **Does** he **like** R&B?	Yes, I **do**. / No, I **don't**. I like country music. Yes, he **does**. / No, he **doesn't**. He like**s** jazz.

What kind of music **do** you **like**?	I	**love** **really like** **like** hip-hop	hip-hop. **a lot**.
What kind of music **don't** you **like**?	I	**don't like** **hate**	pop pop.

For the last block: at all. / very much.

For more information and practice, go to page 137.

8 Match the questions to the answers (a–e).

1 What's your favourite song?

2 Do you like action movies?

3 Who are your favourite singers?

4 What kind of music don't you like?

5 Does your teacher like country music?

a No, she doesn't.

b I hate classical music.

c I love *Clocks* by Coldplay.

d Yes, I do.

e Nicki Minaj and Rihanna.

9 Work in pairs. Answer the questions in Exercise 8 with your own information.

10 ▷ **1.8** Complete the information. Circle the correct words. Listen and check your answers.

SPEAKING Talking about likes and dislikes

11 Write two things you like and one thing you don't like for each category.

Cities	Sports	People's names

12 Listen to your partner's three things. Guess which one your partner doesn't like.

I'll go first: London, Rome and Tokyo.

I think you like Rome and London. You don't like Tokyo.

You're wrong. I don't like London at all. I love Tokyo.

13 Work with another pair. Tell them about your partner's likes and dislikes.

Tyler Spencer lives in Oregon, in the United States. He has an unusual hobby. He ¹*play / plays* the didgeridoo, a traditional instrument from Australia.

Tyler doesn't ²*buy / buys* didgeridoos. He prefers to make his own. His favourite materials to work with ³*is / are* bamboo, oak and other hardwoods.

These days more and more people ⁴*play / plays* the didgeridoo. Oregon's InDidjInUs festival attracts visitors from around the world. Tyler likes the festival ⁵*at all / very much* because he can meet people who share his passion.

Tyler Spencer playing the didgeridoo

1.3 Going viral

1 What does it mean when a video 'goes viral'? Do you know any examples?

TRADITIONAL MUSIC FOR A NEW GENERATION

Teenagers don't often say that they really like folk music. But Sleepy Man Banjo Boys are different – their passion is [1]bluegrass, and they're bringing it to a new [2]generation.

5 The **band** is made up of three teenage brothers from New Jersey, United States – a place which is known more for its rock music. So how did they start playing bluegrass?

The boys were on YouTube one day and saw 10 an old music video of Earl Scruggs – a famous bluegrass musician. '[3]We were like, "Wow, we've never heard anything like this"', says Tommy. The boys listened to some more songs, started learning some **traditional** bluegrass music, and 15 the band was born.

A short time later, they posted a YouTube video of themselves playing music at home. People were **amazed** to see such young boys playing bluegrass so well. The Sleepy Man Banjo Boys' video went viral and millions 20 of people watched it. Just two weeks later, the boys appeared on TV for the first time.

The brothers are now starting to **create** their own kind of bluegrass music, writing their own songs and adding [4]lyrics. 'We're not singing 25 about, you know, the old country road and the [5]barn', explains Tommy. 'I'm not saying that's bad, but we're singing about more **modern** things.'

---

[1] **bluegrass (n)** a type of folk music that started in the United States
[2] **generation (n)** all people of a similar age

[3] **we were like (informal phrase)** = we said
[4] **lyrics (n)** the words to a song
[5] **barn (n)** a building on a farm to keep animals in

Understanding main ideas

2 ▶ **1.9** Read the article quickly. How do the boys become interested in bluegrass?

a They see a music video online.

b Their music teacher loves bluegrass.

c They go to a bluegrass concert.

3 Read the article again. Tick (✓) the things the article mentions.

a where the boys are from

b how the boys became famous

c the boys' favourite song

d the type of things the boys sing about

Understanding details

4 Circle **T** for true or **F** for false.

1 The three boys in the band are school friends.   T   F

2 Sleepy Man Banjo Boys play folk music.   T   F

3 New Jersey is famous for bluegrass music.   T   F

4 Many people watched the band's first YouTube video.   T   F

5 Sleepy Man Banjo Boys make their own bluegrass songs.   T   F

Understanding sequence

5 Number the events in the order they happened (1–6).

a The brothers make a video and put it on YouTube. _____

b The brothers start to learn some bluegrass songs. _____

c The brothers appear on TV. _____

d Many people watch the video. _____

e The brothers start to write their own bluegrass songs. _____

f The brothers watch a YouTube video of a famous bluegrass musician. _1_

Understanding vocabulary

6 Choose the correct options to complete the sentences.

1 An example of a **band** is _____ .
a Earl Scruggs   b Sleepy Man Banjo Boys

2 An example of a **modern** instrument is _____ .
a an electric guitar   b a banjo

3 An example of a **traditional** type of music is _____ .
a country   b rap

4 If you **create** something, you _____ it.
a find   b make

5 If you are **amazed**, you are very _____ .
a happy   b surprised

7 What kinds of traditional music come from your country? What are the traditional instruments?

1.4 Bluegrass virtuosity from ... New Jersey?

TEDTALKS

1 Read the paragraph. Match each **bold** word to its meaning (1-4). You will hear these words in the TED Talk.

> **SLEEPY MAN BANJO BOYS** are from the US **state** of New Jersey – what the boys jokingly call 'the bluegrass **capital** of the **world**'. These young brothers were inspired to teach themselves a new kind of music and share it with the world. Their idea worth spreading is that making music brings equal **joy** to the musicians and the listeners.

1 planet Earth: _____

2 happiness: _____

3 main place for an activity: _____

4 a region of a country: _____

2 ▶ **1.10** Watch the TED Talk. Match each name to the correct age and instrument.

1 Tommy   10   the fiddle

2 Jonny   14   the banjo

3 Robbie   15   the guitar

3 Work in pairs. Look at the photo above. Tell your partner about each person.

> This is Tommy. He's 15 and he plays the guitar.

4 ▶ 1.10 Watch the TED Talk again. How did the band get its name?

   a When Jonny started to play the banjo, he was very little and often fell asleep.

   b When the boys first started playing bluegrass, the music made them feel sleepy.

   c When Jonny first started to play the banjo, it looked like he was sleeping.

CRITICAL THINKING

5 Why does the audience laugh after Tommy says, 'We're three brothers from New Jersey – you know, the bluegrass capital of the world'?

   a It's unusual for brothers to play bluegrass.

   b New Jersey is not at all famous for bluegrass.

   c Bluegrass is popular in the United States but not the rest of the world.

VOCABULARY IN CONTEXT

6 ▶ 1.11 Watch the clips from the TED Talk. Choose the correct meaning of the words.

7 Work in pairs. Complete the sentences in your own words.

   1 When I introduce myself I …

   2 I always feel excited when …

PRESENTATION SKILLS Introducing yourself

TIPS

When you give a presentation, it's sometimes a good idea to introduce yourself. You can give your name and some extra information about your interest in the topic. You can introduce yourself informally or formally.

Informally	Formally
I'm …	I'd like to introduce myself. My name is …

8 ▶ 1.12 Watch Robbie introduce himself. Is his introduction more formal or informal?

9 ▶ 1.12 Watch again. After he gives his name, what other information does he include?

10 Work in a group. Introduce yourself. Include your name and other information.

1.5 Who likes what?

COMMUNICATE Find someone who ...

1 Look at the table. Add one more category to the list.

Find someone who likes ...	Name	Favourite
romantic comedies		
songs in English		
traditional folk music		
rap music		
foreign films		
K-pop		
horror movies		

2 Walk around the classroom. Find someone who likes each thing. Write his or her name and then ask a follow-up question to find out his or her favourite.

3 Work in a group. Share interesting or surprising information you heard.

SHOWING INTEREST

Really? Yeah? Wow! Cool! That's great!

WRITING Introducing yourself by email

4 Read the email and circle the following information.

- Name
- Where from
- Age
- Place of work/studies
- Likes

> Hi Kara,
>
> My name's Teresa. I'm from Tutunendo, Colombia. I'm 19 years old and a first-year student at the University of Medellín. My passion in life is tennis. My favourite tennis player is Serena Williams. I also play tennis every weekend at my local club. I really love it. Write soon!
>
> Teresa

5 Write an email to a classmate. Introduce yourself. Include information about your passion.

2 Spending money

Excited shoppers arrive for a midnight sale in a mall, Oregon, USA

WARM UP

Look at the photo and read the caption. Discuss the questions.

1 Why are the people in the photo running?

2 Do you think people save money when they shop at sales?

3 Do you like shopping in sales? What do you buy?

In this unit you:

- talk about spending money
- describe habits and routines
- watch a TED Talk by **JESSI ARRINGTON**

2.1 Where does my money go?

VOCABULARY Spending money

1 Complete the word map with these words.

bus pass	camera	coffee	concerts	haircuts	shirts

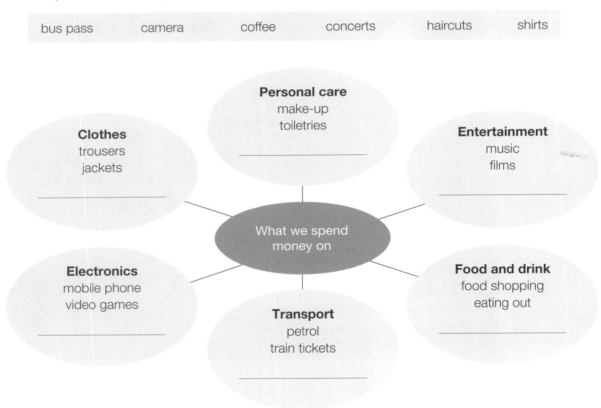

Personal care
make-up
toiletries
_____

Clothes
trousers
jackets
_____

Entertainment
music
films
_____

What we spend
money on

Electronics
mobile phone
video games
_____

Transport
petrol
train tickets
_____

Food and drink
food shopping
eating out
_____

2 Work in pairs. Which of the things in the word map can you buy second-hand?

You can buy video games second-hand.

Yes. And you can buy cameras second-hand too.

LISTENING How I spend my money

> **Listening for negatives**
> When you listen, it's important to be able to hear negative forms. Speakers often use contractions such as:
>
> don't/doesn't   isn't/aren't   can't

3 ▶ **2.1** Listen to Lizzie Nye talk about her spending habits. Tick (✓) the things that Lizzie spends a lot of money on.

a car **c** make-up **e** clothes
b eating out **d** concerts **f** mobile phone

4 ▶ **2.1** Listen again. What does Lizzie say her friends spend a lot of money on? How is Lizzie different? Discuss with a partner.

5 How are you and Lizzie similar? How are you different? Discuss with a partner.

Pronunciation Weak forms (1): *of* and *to*

6 ▶ **2.2** Listen. Notice the pronunciation of the underlined words. Practise saying the sentences.

1 I spend a lot of money going to concerts.
2 It's a bit of a passion of mine.
3 Some of my friends go to restaurants a lot.
4 I prefer to sit and talk to friends face-to-face.

SPEAKING Talking about shopping

7 ▶ **2.3** Listen to the conversation. Where do the two people decide to go shopping?

A: Do you want to go shopping after class?
B: **Sure**. Where do you want to go? **OK / Yeah**
A: Well, I **usually** go to Market Street. They have some great designer shops there. **often / sometimes**
B: Oh. Do you ever go to City Mall?
A: **No, never**. Why? **Hardly ever / Rarely**
B: There's a great second-hand clothes shop there. I go **every week**. **once a week / twice a month**
A: OK, good idea! To be honest, I need to start saving more money.

8 Practise the conversation with a partner. Practise again using the words on the right.

9 Write the names of three places where you shop. Work in pairs. Ask each other about where you shop.

Where do you go shopping?

I sometimes shop at my local market.

Yeah? Why do you like it?

STUDENT SPENDING

A survey on spending habits shows that the average student in the US loves shopping for clothes. The results even suggest that many students spend more money on clothes than they do on food, which may be worrying to some parents!

$$$

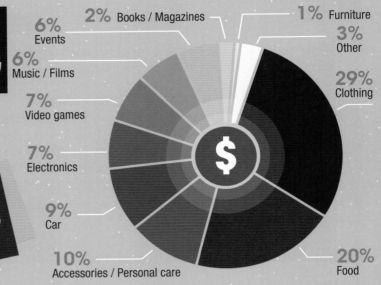

6% Events

2% Books / Magazines

1% Furniture

6% Music / Films

3% Other

7% Video games

29% Clothing

7% Electronics

9% Car

10% Accessories / Personal care

20% Food

GRAMMAR Adverbs and expressions of frequency

1 ▶ 2.4 Look at the infographic. What do students in the United States spend most of their money on?

2 ▶ 2.5 Listen to two people talking about their spending habits. Circle **T** for true or **F** for false.

  1 The boy's spending habits are similar to those shown in the chart.   **T**   **F**

  2 The girl's spending habits are similar to those shown in the chart.   **T**   **F**

3 Read the sentences in the Grammar box. Choose the correct options to complete a and b.

4 Put the sentences in order of frequency from most often (1) to least often (6).

  1 I **usually** buy my food at my local market.

  2 I **never** buy something because I see it in an advert.

  3 I **sometimes** do my food shopping online.

  4 I **hardly ever** buy music.

  5 I **always** buy fair-trade coffee.

  6 I **often** buy new clothes but then decide I don't like them.

5 Change the **adverbs of frequency** in Exercise 4 so the sentences are true for you.

ADVERBS AND EXPRESSIONS OF FREQUENCY

I **hardly ever** buy new clothes.

I go shopping for clothes **every weekend**.

I guess you **usually** buy them second-hand.

I buy two or three new books **every week**.

a Adverbs of frequency (*always, often*, etc.) go *before the verb / at the end of the sentence*.

b Expressions of frequency (*every weekend, twice a week*, etc.) go *before the verb / at the end of the sentence*.

Check your answers on page 138 and do Exercise 1.

LANGUAGE FOCUS Talking about habits and routines

6 ▶ **2.6** Study the examples in the Language focus box.

TALKING ABOUT HABITS AND ROUTINES

Do you **ever** shop online?	Yes, I	always usually often sometimes	shop online.
Do you **ever** buy furniture?	No, I	hardly ever / rarely never	buy furniture.
How often do you go shopping?	I go shopping I **never** go shopping.	every day. once / twice / three times a week.	

For more information and practice, go to page 138.

7 Put the words in the correct order to make questions.

1 ever / you / buy / do / magazines?

2 you / do / ever / online? / shop

3 how / spend / you / do / often / money / on clothes?

4 often / how / you / buy / do / new / shoes?

Pronunciation Intonation in questions

8a ▶ **2.7** Listen and check your answers to Exercise 7. Which questions go up at the end (↑) and which go down (↓)?

8b Work in pairs. Ask and answer the questions in Exercise 7. Answer with your own information.

9 ▶ **2.8** Complete the information. Circle the correct words. Listen and check your answers.

SPEAKING Asking about shopping habits

10 How often do you do these things? Write your answers.

How often do you …
- buy new clothes?
- buy a newspaper or magazine?
- buy coffee in a café?
- buy bottled water?
- download music?
- do a big food shop?

11 Work in pairs. Ask your partner questions to find out their shopping habits.

How often do you buy new clothes?

Let's see. I buy something – a T-shirt or a shirt – about once a month.

When shopping for new clothes, we ¹*ever / usually* think very carefully about the style, the colour and the price. But how ²*often / usually* do you think about the environment?

ECOALF is a clothing company that is trying to help the environment. They make new clothes using recycled materials. They recycle things like old tyres, plastic bottles and ³*hardly ever / sometimes* fishing nets. They even use coffee grounds that they collect from different coffee shops ⁴*once / every* day.

But ECOALF believes that style is important too, so the clothes they make ⁵*never / always* look recycled. In this way, ECOALF hopes people realize that they can help the environment and look good at the same time.

OVER
40
MILLION
PLASTIC
BOTTLES
RECYCLED
SO FAR

ECOALF jackets made from recycled bottles

READING Buy Nothing New Month

1 Read the first paragraph of the article. Do you think the challenge is easy or difficult? Discuss with a partner.

Shoppers at Hell's Kitchen flea market, New York

BUY NOTHING NEW MONTH

Could you live for one month without buying anything new? Buy Nothing New Month started in Australia in 2010. It challenges people once a year to buy nothing new – except food, medicine and
5 **products** used for [1]hygiene – for 30 days.

The aim is to encourage people to be less wasteful and to make us think about the [2]impact our shopping habits have on the **environment**. But the challenge is not simply about [3]going
10 without. People can find other, creative ways to get the things they want. Here are a few examples of how to buy nothing new.

SHOPPING SECOND-HAND

Many people shop for second-hand products
15 at places like charity shops and flea markets. You can usually find a wide variety of items at [4]phenomenal prices, and your money often goes to a good cause. And while you're there, why not **donate** something you no longer use, so someone else can buy it? 20

SWAPPING

With the Internet, **swapping** is easier than ever before. There are many websites, such as swap.com, where you can post a photo of something you don't need. Then, other users 25 can offer something as a swap.

UPCYCLING

Upcycling involves turning something you no longer need into something much more useful. For example, you can turn an empty drink bottle 30 into a beautiful lamp, or an old door into an interesting table.

So why not try the challenge for yourself? You can be a friend to the environment and also to your **wallet**. 35

---

[1] **hygiene (n)** the practice of keeping yourself clean
[2] **impact (n)** effect

[3] **go without (phrasal verb)** to not use or do something
[4] **phenomenal (adj)** really great

Understanding main ideas

2 ▶ **2.9** Read the article. Tick (✓) the true information (a–c).

The article says Buy Nothing New Month makes us think about …

   a the environment.

   b life for poor people.

   c throwing things away.

Understanding examples

3 Find and <u>underline</u> examples of the following in the article.

   1 three types of products you can buy during Buy Nothing New Month

   2 two places where you can buy second-hand products

   3 a website where you can swap items

   4 two examples of upcycling

4 According to the article, which of these items are OK to buy during Buy Nothing New Month?

   a a cup of coffee from a café

   b a bottle of shampoo

   c a new T-shirt for your friend's birthday

   d a new tie for a job interview

   e a computer game from your best friend

5 Tick (✓) the example(s) of upcycling.

   a giving your old clothes to a charity shop

   b fixing a broken table and not throwing it away

   c making a new scarf using old socks

Understanding vocabulary

6 Complete the sentences with these words.

donate   environment   products   swap   wallet

   1 Many people _____ things they don't need to charity shops.

   2 It's OK to buy healthcare _____ during Buy Nothing New Month.

   3 Some people hold parties where they _____ clothes with their friends.

   4 Throwing things away when they are still in good condition is bad for the _____ .

   5 At the end of Buy Nothing New Month, you may have more money than usual in your _____ .

7 Do you think Buy Nothing New Month is a good way to help the environment? Discuss with a partner.

2.4 Wearing nothing new

TEDTALKS

1 Read the paragraph. Match each **bold** word to its meaning (1–4). You will hear these words in the TED Talk.

> **JESSI ARRINGTON** loves wearing crazy, colourful **outfits**. But she never buys new clothes. Instead, she buys **unique** second-hand clothes for her **wardrobe**. Her idea worth spreading is that second-hand shopping can **reduce** our impact on the environment and our wallets, and also be fun and creative.

    1 clothes you wear together: _____

    2 not like any other, special: _____

    3 make less: _____

    4 all the clothes you own: _____

2 ▶ **2.10** Watch Part 1 of the TED Talk. What three things does Jessi Arrington think about when she chooses her outfits? Discuss with a partner.

3 ▶ **2.11** Watch Part 2 of the TED Talk. Match the days of the week with Jessi Arrington's 'life lessons'.

    1 Monday   **a** Be who you are.

    2 Tuesday   **b** Colour is powerful.

    3 Thursday   **c** Develop your own style.

    4 Saturday   **d** Be confident.

CRITICAL THINKING

4 Read the comments* about the TED Talk. Which do you agree with most?

Viewers' comments
M **Mari** – Jessi Arrington says you don't have to spend a lot of money to look great and gives us lots of good examples.
L **LCJ** – She looks great but I think she looks great because she understands colour and fashion. Not everybody has this talent.
P **Paula** – Wow! What a great idea to take an empty suitcase when you go on holiday. I want to try this!

*The comments were created for this activity.

5 Do you agree with this statement of Jessi Arrington's?

'If you think you look good in something, you almost certainly do.'

VOCABULARY IN CONTEXT

6 ▶ 2.12 Watch the clips from the TED Talk. Choose the correct meaning of the words.

7 Work in pairs. Discuss the questions.

    1 What puts you in a bad mood?

    2 Are there any sounds that remind you of childhood?

PRESENTATION SKILLS Using good body language

8 ▶ 2.13 Look at the Presentation tips box. Watch the clip. Tick (✓) the tips that Jessi Arrington follows.

> **TIPS**
>
> Good body language is important. It helps communicate your message and shows you are a confident speaker. Body language includes facial expressions, gestures (how you move your hands) and how you stand. Try these tips:
>
> **1** Keep your body open. Try not to cross your arms or legs.
>
> **2** Stand up straight.
>
> **3** Gesture with your hands open.
>
> **4** Make eye contact with the audience.
>
> **5** Smile.

9 ▶ 2.13 Watch again. What else does Jessi Arrington do (or not do) that shows she's confident?

10 Work in a group. Stand up and tell the group a little about yourself. Try to use good body language.

27

2.5 How green are you?

COMMUNICATE Doing a quiz

1 Are you a green shopper? Read the questions and mark your answers.

How often do you …	Never	Sometimes	Often
1 buy locally produced products?	☐	☐	☐
2 take a reusable cloth bag to a shop?	☐	☐	☐
3 buy products made from recycled materials?	☐	☐	☐
4 buy second-hand items?	☐	☐	☐
5 donate to charity shops?	☐	☐	☐
6 recycle the packaging that comes with your products?	☐	☐	☐
7 travel to the shops by car?	☐	☐	☐

2 Work in pairs. Take turns asking and answering the questions.

3 Look back at the quiz. Circle how green you think your partner is.

very green	green	quite green	not very green

4 Work in a group. Tell the group how green you think your partner is. Give reasons.

ADDING EXTRA INFORMATION

Jamie rides his bike when he goes shopping **and** he cycles to work.

I sometimes donate to charity shops. **Plus / Also**, I often buy my clothes at charity shops.

I think Kate is a very green shopper. **What's more**, she buys a lot of things second-hand.

WRITING Sharing information online

5 Read the post. What does the person want?

Help! I want to buy some second-hand items, such as clothes, music, comic books and furniture. Where's a good place to shop? All ideas welcome. Thanks!

6 Read this response to the post. Then write your own response to the post. Include the name of the shop, what it sells, how often you go there and what you like about it.

For furniture, there's a great shop on Castle Street. It's called Couch Potato. They sell cheap second-hand furniture. I usually go there during the week when it's not very busy.

3 Jobs

A staff member looks at live data from social media at an exhibition, London, UK

WARM UP

Look at the photo and read the caption. Discuss the questions.

1 What do you think the woman in the photo wants to find out?

2 Do you think this looks like an interesting job? Why?

3 Can you think of other 'new' jobs from the last ten years?

In this unit you:

- talk about jobs
- describe different jobs
- watch a TED Talk by **CHRIS BURKARD**

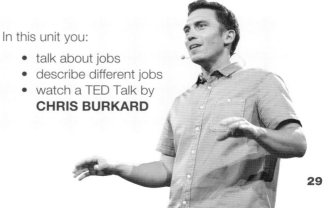

French chef Eric Cros shows students how to prepare lamb and vegetables

3.1 What do you do?

VOCABULARY Jobs

1 ▶ **3.1** Complete the sentences using these words. Listen and check your answers.

chef	journalist	photographer	teacher
dancer	manager	scientist	waiter

1 A _____ takes pictures with a camera.

2 A _____ makes meals in a restaurant.

3 A _____ writes for a newspaper.

4 A _____ often performs on a stage.

5 A _____ works with children in a school.

6 A _____ often does experiments.

7 A _____ works with people in an office.

8 A _____ serves food and drinks.

2 Work in pairs. Make sentences about the jobs in Exercise 1 using people you know or famous people.

My brother is a waiter.

Stephen Hawking is a scientist.

LISTENING A fun job

Listening selectively
You may not understand every word when people speak.
Listen selectively and focus on the key information you need.

3 ▶ **3.2** Listen to an interview with journalist and TV presenter Richard Lenton. Tick (✓) the topics that he talks about.

a the best thing about his job   **c** his future hopes

b the challenges in his job   **d** his free time

4 ▶ **3.2** Listen again. Circle the correct words.

1 Richard usually presents *soccer / tennis* programmes.

2 Richard *likes / doesn't like* sport.

3 The World Cup was a challenge because he worked *at night / with famous people.*

4 Richard usually plays soccer *once / twice* a week.

_____
soccer = football

Richard Lenton (right)
interviews David Beckham

Pronunciation Word linking (1)

5a ▶ **3.3** Listen. Notice how we link some words when we say them together.

Can you tell‿us‿about your job?

5b ▶ **3.4** Listen to these sentences. Mark the words that link together. Practise saying the sentences.

1 I'm a TV host and journalist.

2 I'm working in sport, which is my life and passion.

3 It was the best experience of my working life.

4 I would like to play more than one game a week.

SPEAKING Talking about jobs

6 ▶ **3.5** Listen to the conversation. Does speaker B like his new job?

A: So, how do you like being a barista?

B: Oh, it's **great**!   fantastic / excellent

A: Yeah? What do you do every day?

B: Well, you know, I make coffee and serve it to customers.

A: Is it **hard work**?   difficult / tough

B: Sometimes. **The hours aren't** great, but I don't mind.   The pay isn't / The boss isn't

A: Isn't it boring?

B: No, it's really **fun**. I meet a lot of cool people.   interesting / enjoyable

7 Practise the conversation with a partner. Practise again using the words on the right.

8 Imagine you have a new job. Choose one from this lesson or think of your own. Work in pairs. Ask each other about your jobs.

Do you have a job?   Yes! I am a chef at China Bistro.

3.2 What's your job like?

TOP 10 DREAM JOBS

A recent survey asked 3,000 workers in the UK to name their dream job. For many people, the perfect job is a pilot. Others prefer jobs in the arts – such as a writer or an actor – or in sport.

1 Pilot
2 Charity worker
3 Writer
4 Photographer
5 Musician
6 Sports trainer
7 Racing car driver
8 Actor
9 Journalist
10 Artist

GRAMMAR *like* and *would like*

1 ▶ 3.6 Look at the infographic. Is the information surprising?

2 ▶ 3.7 Listen to two people talking about jobs. Complete the sentences.

  1 The woman works as a _____ .

  2 She doesn't like the _____ .

  3 She'd like to be a _____ .

3 Read the sentences in the Grammar box. Choose the correct options to complete a–d.

LIKE AND WOULD LIKE

I **don't like** being a journalist.

I really **don't like** the hours.

I'**d** really **like** to be a charity worker.

a Use *like / would like* to talk about now.

b Use *like / would like* to talk about the future.

c *Like / would like* is followed by a noun or *-ing*

d *Like / would like* is followed by *to* + infinitive

Check your answers on page 139 and do Exercise 1.

4 Choose the correct options to complete the conversations.

  1 A: In the UK many people *like / would like* to be a pilot.

    B: Really? I *wouldn't / don't*.

  2 A: *Would / Do* you like to be a musician?

    B: Yes, I *would / do*. I'd love to be a rock musician.

  3 A: *Does / Would* your brother like being a photographer?

    B: Yes, he *does / would*. He says it's a great job.

  4 A: Do you like *to be / being* a teacher?

    B: Yes, I *like / would like* it a lot but it's hard work.

  5 A: Some people say they would love *to be / being* an actor.

    B: Really? *I'd like / I like* to be a singer.

  6 A: I'm a chef but I *don't like / wouldn't like* working in the evenings.

    B: What job *would you / do you* like to do?

LANGUAGE FOCUS Asking about and describing jobs

5 ▶ **3.8** Study the examples in the Language focus box.

ASKING ABOUT AND DESCRIBING JOBS

Do you **have** a job?

What do you **do**?

What's your job **like**?

What do you **like** about your job?
What don't you **like** about your job?
What (kind of) job **would** you **like** to have (one day)?

For more information and practice, go to page 139.

Yes, I **do**.
No, I **don't**. I'm a student.

I'm a manager.
I **work** in marketing.

It's (really) fun.
It's (pretty) easy.

The pay **is** great.

I **don't like** the hours. They're terrible.

I'd like to be a charity worker.

6 Match the questions to the answers (a–e).

   1 Do you have a job?
   2 What do you do?
   3 What's your job like?
   4 What don't you like about your job?
   5 What job would you like to have one day?

   a It's pretty easy.
   b Yes, I do.
   c I'm a fashion designer.
   d I'd love to write for a magazine.
   e The hours are very long.

7 ▶ **3.9** Complete the information. Circle the correct words. Then listen and check your answers.

Pronunciation /dju:/

8a ▶ **3.10** Listen. Notice how *do you* sounds in this sentence. Practise saying the sentence.

Do you like your job?

8b ▶ **3.11** Listen to the questions from Exercise 6 and underline the /dju:/ sounds. Which sentences don't have this sound?

SPEAKING Talking about a future job

9 Think of three jobs you'd like to have and give reasons.

10 Work in a group. Share the jobs you'd like to have. Respond with questions and opinions.

I'd love to be a chef.   Why is that?

Many people ¹*do / would* like to work as a pilot one day. In the UK, it's the number one dream job. But what's the job really ²*like / love*? A good point is you can travel to a lot of interesting places – for free. The pay is ³*like / pretty* good too. So what ⁴*doesn't / don't* pilots like about their job? The hours ⁵*are / is* not great – they're often away from home, and spend a lot of time in hotels. Pilots often ⁶*work / works* on holidays too, as those are very busy days for flying.

Ethiopian Airlines's first female captain, Amsale Gualu

3.3 Never too old

READING A dancer's dream

1 Look at the title, photo and caption. What do you think the article is mainly about?

    a why it is important to start ballet training early

    b the challenges someone had before becoming a dancer

    c the reason more boys are becoming interested in ballet

2 ▶ 3.12 Read the article. Check your prediction.

Misty Copeland performing for the American Ballet Theatre

A DANCER'S DREAM

An athletic young woman turns, spins and leaps. In the background, a young girl reads a ¹rejection letter from a ballet school. 'You have the wrong body for ballet', it says, 'and at thirteen,
5 you are too old.' This was one of the most popular advertisements of 2014, and **features** American Ballet Theatre's ²principal dancer Misty Copeland.

This was not a real letter. But Copeland says it is
10 very similar to letters from her childhood. While many dancers start at the age of three, Copeland only began to study ballet as a thirteen-year-old. People often told her that she was too old, or that she didn't have the **perfect** body type (she is only
15 157 cm tall). Her family moved a lot, and it was sometimes a **struggle** to attend ballet classes.

But Copeland loved dancing and did not want to **quit**. She stayed with her ballet teacher during the week and spent time with her family only at the weekend. This was a 20 difficult **routine**, but she worked hard and won her first national ³competition when she was fourteen years old. Copeland joined the American Ballet Theatre in 2000 and performed in many ballets over the next few 25 years. In 2007, she became a ⁴solo performer, and in 2015 she became its principal dancer.

Copeland is now a dancer, author and Broadway performer. She also stars in the 2015 film *A Ballerina's Tale*. So what's next? According to 30 Copeland, anything is possible: 'My **career** really is just now beginning.'

---

¹ **rejection (n)** saying no to someone who applies for a job or place of study

² **principal (adj)** most important

³ **competition (n)** an event to find out who is the best at something

⁴ **solo (adj)** done alone, not with other people

Understanding sequence

3 Complete the timeline with information about Misty Copeland.

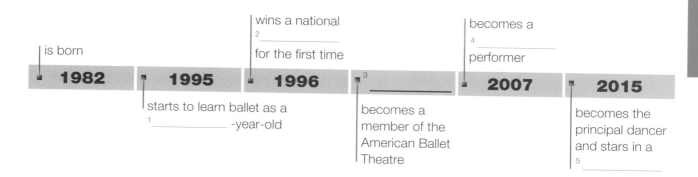

is born

1982

starts to learn ballet as a
1_____ -year-old

1995

wins a national
2_____
for the first time

1996

3_____

becomes a
member of the
American Ballet
Theatre

becomes a
4_____
performer

2007

2015

becomes the
principal dancer
and stars in a
5_____

Understanding details

4 Tick (✓) each challenge the article talks about.

   a Many people told Copeland she was too old to start ballet.

   b Copeland's ballet classes were very expensive.

   c Many people said Copeland had the wrong body type to be a ballerina.

   d Copeland's family often moved house so it was difficult to go to ballet classes.

   e Copeland had problems with her school work.

   f Copeland had to spend a lot of time away from her family.

Understanding vocabulary

5 Match the words in **bold** from the article to their definitions.

   1 **perfect**   a having all the qualities you want

   2 **struggle**   b the usual things you do

   3 **routine**   c something that is very difficult to do

6 Choose the correct options to complete the definitions.

   1 If an advertisement **features** someone _____ .

      a this person is in the advertisement

      b the advertisement describes this person

   2 If you **quit** something, you _____ doing it.

      a start

      b stop

   3 An example of a **career** is working _____ .

      a in a part-time summer job

      b as a full-time business manager

7 Which of Misty Copeland's struggles do you think was the biggest challenge?
   Discuss with a partner.

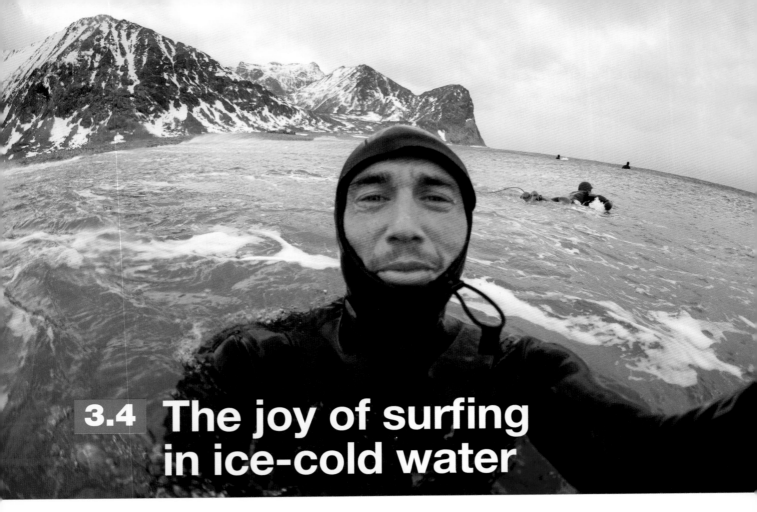

3.4 The joy of surfing in ice-cold water

TEDTALKS

1 Read the paragraph. Match each **bold** word to its meaning (1–4). You will hear these words in the TED Talk.

CHRIS BURKARD is a surf photographer, but you won't find him working on a warm **exotic** island. He prefers the Arctic, with its **rough** seas and **freezing** temperatures. His idea worth spreading is that interesting activities are also sometimes difficult, but the **suffering** gives your work more meaning and gives you more joy.

1 very cold: _____   **3** unusual or different: _____

2 not calm: _____   **4** pain: _____

2 ▶ 3.13 Watch Part 1 of the TED Talk and answer the questions.

1 Where is Chris Burkard in the photo?

a Canada   b Iceland   c Norway

2 How does he describe the water?

a beautiful   b freezing   c rough

3 ▶ 3.14 Watch Part 2 of the talk. Put the events in Chris Burkard's life in the correct order (1–4).

a He begins to work in cold places.   _____

b He begins to work in warm places.   _____

c He finds his job boring.   _____

d He learns that sometimes what we enjoy is also a struggle.   _____

CRITICAL THINKING

4 Read the comment* about the TED Talk. What does the viewer think Chris Burkard loves about his job? Do you agree?

> **Viewer's comment**
>
> **S** **SalW** – Chris Burkard loves his job because he can go to places that other people don't get to! I'd love to have a job like that.

The comment was created for this activity.

5 Tick (✓) the other reasons you think Chris Burkard loves his job.

a beautiful nature   **c** it's also his hobby   **e** the challenge

b adventure   **d** being cold   **f** the photography

6 Does Chris Burkard make you want to be an Arctic surf photographer. Why? / Why not? Write your own comment.

VOCABULARY IN CONTEXT

7 ▶ **3.15** Watch the clips from the TED Talk. Choose the correct meaning of the words.

8 Work in pairs. Discuss the questions.

    1 Can you describe what happened on your last 'big' birthday?

    2 Where would you like to go on a trip? Why?

PRESENTATION SKILLS Thanking the audience

TIPS

At the end of your presentation, it's important to thank the audience for listening. There may also be opportunities during the presentation, for example if the audience claps you.

9 ▶ **3.16** Watch the clip. Write the phrase Chris Burkard uses to thank the audience.

10 ▶ **3.17** Watch two clips from the TED Talks from units 1 and 2. Tick (✓) how each speaker thanks the audience.

	Thank you	Thank you so much	Thank you very much
Sleepy Man Banjo Boys			
Jessi Arrington			

11 Work in a group. Think of other ways to thank the audience.

3.5 It's my dream job

COMMUNICATE Guessing the job

1 Look at these jobs. Look up any you don't know in your dictionary.

airline pilot	film actor	professional athlete	TV chef
café barista	graphic artist	songwriter	university lecturer
dog trainer	photojournalist	surfing instructor	video game designer

2 ▶ **3.18** Listen to five sentences describing one of the jobs in Exercise 1. After each sentence, try to guess which job it is.

3 Work in pairs. Student A: Turn to page 149. Student B: Turn to page 152. Take turns to guess your partner's job.

4 Now think of your dream job. Write five sentences to describe the job. Use the language from Exercises 1 and 2 to help you.

5 Work in groups of three or four. Take turns to read your job descriptions. Your group members must try to guess the job you are describing.

ASKING FOR CLARIFICATION

When you don't understand what someone says in English, it's OK to check or ask them to repeat it.

Can you repeat that, please?

I'm sorry. What did you say?

Can you say that again?

Did you say … ?

WRITING Describing a dream job

6 Read the blog post. Complete the text with these linking words.

also	and	because	but

I work as a dog trainer. I teach dogs to behave well _____ to follow instructions. It's fun _____ challenging. I enjoy it _____ I love animals. _____ , I enjoy meeting new people.

7 Answer the questions about the blog post.

1 What does she do?

2 What three things does she like about it?

8 Imagine you have your dream job. Write a blog post about what you do, and why you like it. Use linking words.

Presentation 1 | UNITS 1–3

MODEL PRESENTATION

1 Read the transcript of Paula's presentation. Complete the text with these words.

favourite	much	people	work
goes	name	tell	works

'Hi. My ¹_____'s Paula. I'd like to ²_____ you a bit about my brother, Zak. He's 21 and he's a university student. He also ³_____ part-time as a barista. The pay isn't great and he says it's hard ⁴_____ but he really enjoys it. He also really loves fashion and shopping for clothes. He ⁵_____ shopping every weekend and his ⁶_____ shop is Uniqlo. He has an interesting hobby, too. He's an actor for a local theatre group. He really loves acting – he says it's fun and he meets a lot of ⁷_____. One day, he'd like to write his own plays. OK, so that's my brother Zak! Thank you so ⁸_____ for listening.'

2 ▶ P.1 Watch the presentation and check your answers.

3 ▶ P.1 Review the list of presentation skills from units 1–3. Which does the speaker use? Tick (✓) them as you watch again.

Presentation skills: units 1–3
The speaker:
• introduces himself/herself ☐
• smiles ☐
• stands up straight ☐
• makes eye contact ☐
• thanks the audience ☐

4 Look at the notes Paula made before her presentation. Did she forget to say anything?

- Introduction: my name / topic
- Zak: 21 / student / studies Art
- His job: barista / pay / hard work / enjoy
- Likes: fashion / shopping every weekend / Uniqlo
- Hobby: actor / theatre group / fun / meets people
- Dreams: write own play / star in a film
- End: thank audience

YOUR TURN!

5 Plan a short presentation to introduce someone you know. Use Paula's notes from Exercise 4 for ideas and include any other information. Make notes on a card or a small piece of paper.

6 Look at the Useful phrases box. Think about which phrases you need in your presentation.

USEFUL PHRASES

Introducing yourself

(Informally) I'm / My name's …

(Formally) I want / I'd like to introduce myself. I am / My name is …

Introducing your topic

I'd like to tell you / talk to you about …

Describing likes / favourites

He/She really likes/loves/enjoys …

His/Her favourite sport is …

Describing routines

He/She goes running every week / twice a month.

Describing dreams

One day, he'd/she'd like to be a sports trainer.

Ending

Thank you so much (for listening).

Thanks for listening.

7 Work in pairs. Take turns to give your presentation using your notes. Use some of the presentation skills from units 1–3. As you listen, tick (✓) each skill your partner uses.

Presentation skills: units 1–3	
The speaker:	
• introduces himself/herself	☐
• smiles	☐
• stands up straight	☐
• makes eye contact	☐
• thanks the audience	☐

8 Use your checklist to give your partner some feedback on their talk. Try to include good things, and one thing they can improve.

> Well done! You introduced yourself and you smiled a lot. But you didn't thank the audience.

4 Talents

Marc Yu and Lang Lang play the piano at a concert, California, USA

WARM UP

Look at the photo and read the caption. Discuss the questions.

1 How would you describe the musicians in the photo?

2 What qualities do you need to become a professional musician?

3 How do you feel about performing in public?

In this unit you:

- talk about activities
- describe abilities and talents
- watch a TED Talk by **TOM THUM**

A contestant finishes his sand sculpture during a competition at Revere Beach in the United States

4.1 What are you good at?

VOCABULARY Activities

1 Look at the activities. ~~Cross out~~ the option that doesn't belong.

1 playing	friends	football	video games
2 taking	photos	tests	presentations
3 making	decisions	photos	friends
4 giving	advice	decisions	presentations

2 Choose six activities from Exercise 1. How good are you at each of them? Write them on the scale below. Then think about two more activities and add them to the scale.

←————————————————————————→

Really bad   Not very good   Good   Pretty good   Very good

3 Work in pairs. Share your information.

I'm pretty good at playing football. How about you?

I'm not very good at playing football.

LISTENING A unique ability

> **Recognizing unstressed words**
> Native speakers do not stress every word they say. It's important to be able to recognize the sounds of unstressed words. For example, the word *can* is usually not stressed.

4 ▶ **4.1** Listen to the information about Okotanpe, a contact juggler. Circle the correct option.

Contact jugglers can …

a play the piano and juggle.   **c** juggle with bubbles.
b roll balls on their bodies.

5 ▶ **4.1** Listen again. Circle **T** for true or **F** for false.

1 Many people watch Okotanpe on YouTube.   T   F
2 The balls are very soft.   T   F
3 Okotanpe practises every day.   T   F
4 Okotanpe can also do magic tricks.   T   F

Okotanpe is a contact juggler from Japan.

Pronunciation /ɪ/ and /iː/

6a ▶ **4.2** Listen to the pronunciation of the long /iː/ and short /ɪ/ sounds in this sentence.

H<u>e</u> has a un<u>i</u>que ab<u>i</u>l<u>i</u>t<u>y</u>.

6b ▶ **4.3** Look at the sounds in bold in these extracts. Listen and double underline the long /iː/ sounds. Listen again and single underline the short /ɪ/ sounds. Practise saying the sentences.

1 H**e**'s very good at **i**t.
2 H**e** has many popular v**i**deos.
3 h**i**s amaz**i**ng skills
4 H**e** can make **i**t look very **ea**sy.

SPEAKING Talking about abilities

7 ▶ **4.4** Listen to the conversation. What is speaker B good at?

A: Wow! You're **pretty good.**   **really good / not bad**
B: Thanks. I practise a lot.
A: Can you play any other instruments?
B: Well, I can play the guitar – but I'm not **very good** at it.   **great / that good**
A: Do you know how to read music?
B: Actually, no. I'm **really bad** at it.   **hopeless / terrible**
A: Really? So how do you learn the songs?
B: I usually just listen and then try to play what I hear.
A: Wow! That's **amazing.**   **great / fantastic**

8 Practise the conversation with a partner. Practise again using the words on the right.

9 Write two true and two false statements about things you are good at. Work in a group. Share your information. Can others guess which statements are false?

OK, I'll go first. I'm really good at singing.   Hmm. I think that's true.

Sorry, you're wrong. I'm really bad at it.

4.2 Can you stand on your head?

TURNING TALENT INTO CASH
Do you have a unique talent? There's a job out there waiting for you!

Pearl diver
Are you good at swimming underwater? Can you hold your breath for a long time? Pearl divers earn money by collecting pearls from the bottom of the sea.

Human statue
Perhaps your only ability is that you can stand perfectly still. Well, there's still a job for you! You can get paid for dressing up as a statue in public as part of promotional events.

Odour tester
Some people even make a career out of a good sense of smell. Odour testers make a living by testing the smell of things, like perfumes and deodorants.

Voice artist
If you can speak in different, funny voices, how about becoming a voice artist? Providing voices for characters in animations can get you a pretty good salary.

GRAMMAR *can* and *can't*

1 ▶ **4.5** Look at the infographic. Do you think you can do any of these jobs?

2 ▶ **4.6** Listen to two people talking about jobs. Complete the sentences.

1 The man doesn't know how to _____ .
2 The woman is good at _____ .
3 The woman can't swim _____ very well.
4 The man can _____ in funny voices.

3 Read the sentences in the Grammar box. Choose the correct options to complete a and b.

CAN AND CAN'T

Well it sounds fun, but I **can't** swim.

I **can** speak in funny voices and I love acting.

a Sentence 1 describes an ability you *have / don't have*.

b Sentence 2 describes an ability you *have / don't have*.

Check your answers on page 140 and do Exercises 1–2.

---

4 Look at this list of someone's skills. Write sentences using *can* or *can't*.

1 take good photographs ✓
  I can take good photographs.
2 play the guitar ✗
  _____
3 write interesting stories ✓
  _____
4 dance ✓
  _____
5 drive a car ✗
  _____
6 make good coffee ✓
  _____

Pronunciation *can* and *can't*

5a ▶ **4.7** Listen to the different ways we pronounce *can* and *can't*.

Can you take good photographs? /ə/
Yes, I **can**. /æ/
No, I **can't**. /ɑː/

5b Work in pairs. Make questions from the prompts in Exercise 4. Give your own short answers. Try to use the correct pronunciation of *can* and *can't*.

Can you play the guitar?

No, I can't.

LANGUAGE FOCUS Describing abilities and talents

6 ▶ **4.8** Study the examples in the Language focus box.

DESCRIBING ABILITIES AND TALENTS

Are you **good at**	**languages**? **writing** essays?	Yes, **I am**. No, **I'm not**.
Do you **know how to**	**read** Japanese? **speak** Spanish?	Yes, I **do**. No, I **don't**.
Can you	**play** a musical instrument? **ride** a bike?	Yes, I **can**. No, I **can't**.

What abilities or **talents do** you **have**?	I **can**	**speak** Spanish **fluently**. **solve** word problems **easily**. **read** Korean **well**. **run fast**.

For more information and practice, go to page 140.

7 Complete each question with one word.

1 Do you _____ how to say 'hello' in Chinese?
2 Are you _____ at writing essays?
3 _____ you hold your breath for one minute?
4 Are you good _____ swimming underwater?
5 _____ you play the piano?
6 Do you know _____ to count to ten in French?

8 Work in pairs. Ask and answer the questions in Exercise 7.

9 ▶ **4.9** Complete the information with these words. One word is extra. Listen and check your answers.

can	easily	do
good	doing	well

SPEAKING A talented class

10 Complete the list of questions with two more abilities or talents.

- Can you say the alphabet backwards?
- Can you stand on one foot for 20 seconds?
- Do you know how to say 'hello' in German?
- Can you touch your toes without bending your knees?
- Can you sing 'Happy Birthday' in English?
- Do you know how to _____?
- Can you _____?

11 Walk around the class and ask the questions. Make the person *show* you the ability. Find one person for each ability.

OK, can you say the alphabet backwards?

Yeah, I think so. I'll show you.

Arthur Benjamin is a maths lecturer. But he also has a second job – as a 'mathemagician'.

As you can guess, Benjamin is very [1]_____ at maths. But he also knows how to [2]_____ magic, and he combines his two passions into amazing performances.

Benjamin is really good at [3]_____ difficult maths quickly. During his performances, Benjamin invites audience members with calculators on stage. He races them to see who [4]_____ solve a difficult maths problem first. Benjamin wins [5]_____ almost every time.

Arthur Benjamin performs 'mathemagic'

4.3 Not all fun and games

READING Pro gaming: a dream career?

1 Work in pairs. Discuss the questions.

1 Do you use your talents and interests in your job?

2 What is the perfect job for your talents and interests?

A good job for me is food critic because I love eating and writing.

Fans watch a StarCraft II tournament in Seoul, South Korea

PRO GAMING: A DREAM CAREER?

1 Playing video games and getting money for it seems like a dream career for many of today's teenagers. But is it all fun and games?

Big business

5 **2** Pro gaming is certainly big business. In 2015, there were more than 3,000 gaming **tournaments** and over 10,000 professional players worldwide. Many tournaments attract huge online audiences, and successful gamers can earn millions of dollars 10 from prize money and **advertisements**. The industry is clearly [1]thriving.

What it takes

3 Becoming a professional is not just about being good at playing games – it also takes a lot 15 of hard work. Some pro gamers practise for fourteen hours a day. 'You need to dedicate pretty much your whole life to it', says ex-gamer George 'HotshotGG' Georgallidis.

Not all fun and games

4 It can be a difficult job as well. **Stress** is a big 20 issue for gamers. [2]Fatigue is another, and **injuries** are common. Top player Hai Lam suffered [3]wrist problems after years of pro gaming. Careers are short, and many gamers **retire** before they are 30 and struggle to find another job. 25

5 However, the bad points probably won't change the dreams of many teenage gamers. And angry parents are still likely to hear the [4]excuse, 'But I'm just practising for my future job!'

---

[1] **thrive (v)** to do well

[2] **fatigue (n)** being extremely tired

[3] **wrist (n)** the joint between your hand and your arm

[4] **excuse (n)** a reason to explain why you did something wrong

Understanding purpose

2 ▶ **4.10** Read the article. Choose the option that describes the main purpose of each paragraph.

Paragraph 2

a to describe how pro gaming tournaments work

b to show how big the pro gaming industry is these days

Paragraph 3

a to explain how pro gamers practise for major tournaments

b to describe the hard work needed to be a pro gamer

Paragraph 4

a to describe the difficult parts of being a pro gamer

b to explain the career of a retired pro gamer

Understanding supporting details

3 Find and underline the following supporting details in the article.

1 three examples of how pro gaming is now 'big business'

2 the amount of practice some pro gamers do

3 three examples of the difficult parts of being a pro gamer

Understanding vocabulary

4 Complete the table showing the advantages and disadvantages of a career as a pro gamer. Use the words in the box.

advertisements   injuries   retire   stress   tournaments

A career as a pro gamer	
Advantages	Disadvantages
• You can earn a lot of money by winning ¹_____ and through ²_____ . • You can have a career doing something you love.	• You need to practise a lot. • Some gamers get ³_____ that stop them from playing. • Many pro gamers have to ⁴_____ early and find another job. • ⁵_____ is also a problem for many pro gamers.

5 Do you think professional gaming is a good career choice? Why? / Why not? Discuss with a partner.

I think it's a good career choice because …

4.4 The orchestra in my mouth

TEDTALKS

1 Read the paragraph. Match each **bold** word to its meaning (1–4). You will hear these words in the TED Talk.

> **TOM THUM** has an interesting talent. He is a beatboxer. This means he can make unusual **sounds** with his **voice**. His idea worth spreading is that our talents can **allow** us to **pursue** amazing and sometimes surprising careers.

1 follow, have: _____

3 what we hear: _____

2 the sound when you speak: _____

4 let, make it possible for: _____

2 ▶ 4.11 Watch Part 1 of the TED Talk. Circle the correct options to complete the sentences.

   1 Tom Thum makes sounds using *his voice alone / his voice and microphone effects*.

   2 He does most of his performances *in / outside* Brisbane.

3 ▶ 4.12 Watch Part 2 of the TED Talk. Tick (✓) the things that Tom Thum says the technology allows him to do.

   a sound like a musical instrument

   c play his voice backwards

   b mix sounds together

   d play his voice over and over again

4 ▶ 4.13 Watch Part 3 of the TED Talk. What kind of music does Tom Thum perform?

CRITICAL THINKING

5 Which do you think needs most talent and most practice – using your own voice or playing an instrument? Discuss with a partner.

VOCABULARY IN CONTEXT

6 ▶ **4.14** Watch the clips from the TED Talk. Choose the correct meaning of the words.

7 Work in pairs. Discuss the questions.

1 What do you do when you have time on your hands?

2 What is your favourite journey? What do you like about it?

PRESENTATION SKILLS Introducing a topic

Introducing the topic helps the audience know what to expect and helps the speaker structure the talk. Here are some useful phrases.

I'm going to discuss …   I'd like to share with you …
I want to show you …   I'd like to give you some perspective on …
I want to tell you about …   I'd like to give a demonstration of …

8 ▶ **4.15** Watch the clips. How does Tom Thum introduce his topic? Complete the sentences.

1 'I'd _____ to give you guys a bit of a _____ about what I do.'

2 'I would _____ to _____ with you some technology that I brought …'

9 ▶ **4.16** Complete the sentences. Write **a, b** or **c**. Watch the clips to check your answers.

1 **Robbie Mizzone (Sleepy Man Banjo Boys)**: 'I'm just going to _____.'

2 **Jessi Arrington**: 'I'd really love to _____.'

3 **Chris Burkard**: 'I would love to _____.'

a give you a little perspective on what a day in my life can look like

b take a second to introduce the band

c show you my week's worth of outfits right now

10 Choose one of these topics. Give a one-minute talk on that topic to your partner. Remember to introduce the topic first.

a talented person you know   a job you'd like   someone who has a job they love

49

4.5 Are you right for the job?

COMMUNICATE Interviewing for a job

1 Work in pairs. Read the information. Then try the roleplay.

Student A: You work for an employment agency. You want to find people for some jobs. Interview Student B using the questions on page 151. Ask for extra information. Write down your partner's answers.

Student B: You need a job. Student A works for an employment agency. Answer his or her questions.

CONVERSATION FILLERS

It's fine to take some time to think during a conversation. But it's important to let the other person know you're thinking. In English, people often make these sounds:

| Well … | Um … | Let's see … | Hmm … |

2 Now change roles.

3 Turn to page 151 and look at the list of job vacancies. Think about your partner's abilities and likes. Find two or more jobs you think are good for your partner.

4 Tell your partner about the jobs you think are good for him or her. Does your partner agree?

Underwater photographer is a good job for you. You said you're good with animals, and you can swim well.

OK. Yes, that sounds interesting. Anything else?

WRITING Describing an unusual ability

5 Think about the people you know. Who has an unusual ability or talent?

Person: _____

Ability/Talent: _____

6 Read the paragraph. Then write your own paragraph about the person you know.

My uncle is very talented. He can play the bagpipes. They are a traditional musical instrument from Scotland. He sometimes plays them at birthday parties or other events, but he usually just plays them for fun.

5 Technology

A company in California uses iPads and telepresence robots to communicate with staff in Moscow

WARM UP

Look at the photo and read the caption. Discuss the questions.

1 How does the company in the photo use technology?

2 Do you think this is a good way to do business?

3 Do you think new technology makes people good at communicating?

In this unit you:
- talk about gadgets
- describe how things work
- watch a TED Talk by **YVES ROSSY**

More and more people now own a personal drone

5.1 I can't live without it

VOCABULARY Gadgets

1 Read these paragraphs. Write each **bold** word next to its opposite (1–8).

Most smartwatches have a very cool, **modern** design. They're **easy to use** and link with your smartphone so you get all your messages as **fast** as possible.	While many people still buy books, others prefer e-readers. Recent models are extremely **light** and **thin**, but they're also very **strong**. You can download books directly to your device.	Personal drones are becoming more and more popular. They're great **fun** and easy to fly. But they can be **expensive** – from £200 and up.

1 boring ≠ _____   **5** old-fashioned ≠ _____

2 cheap ≠ _____   **6** slow ≠ _____

3 difficult to use ≠ _____   **7** thick ≠ _____

4 heavy ≠ _____   **8** weak ≠ _____

2 How important are these gadgets to you? Write your opinion (1–4) about each one.

> 1 = I can't live without mine.   3 = I'd like to get one.
> 2 = I like having one.   4 = I don't need one.

_____ a smartphone   _____ a smart TV

_____ a game console   _____ a smartwatch

_____ a tablet   _____ a personal drone

_____ an e-reader   _____ a fitness band

3 Work in pairs. Share your opinions.

I can't live without my game console.

Really? I don't need one. I play games on my tablet.

LISTENING How I used drones to make an amazing video

Listening for attitude
In order to understand a speaker's attitude or opinion about something, listen for positive or negative words or phrases. Sometimes a speaker's tone can also help.

Sam Cossman in Vanuatu

4 ▶ **5.1** Listen to the information about National Geographic explorer Sam Cossman. What did he study in Vanuatu? Circle the correct answer.

a a giant cave   **b** a volcano   **c** a temple

5 ▶ **5.1** Listen again. Circle the correct options.

1 Cossman used drones to *take images / measure the temperature*.

2 Some drones were destroyed because of the *strong winds / heat*.

3 Cossman also used a special *suit / car* to get close.

4 Cossman said he *was / wasn't* terrified during his experience.

Pronunciation Sentence stress

6 ▶ **5.2** Listen. Notice how the <u>important</u> words are stressed in each sentence. Work in pairs. Practise saying the sentences. Remember to stress the key words.

1 In <u>twenty</u> <u>fifteen</u>, <u>Sam</u> <u>Cossman</u> visited <u>Vanuatu</u> on a <u>project</u> to <u>study</u> an <u>active</u> <u>volcano</u>.

2 <u>Cossman</u> and his <u>team</u> learned <u>a lot</u> about this <u>amazing</u> <u>place</u>.

3 They <u>also</u> took some <u>great</u> <u>photos</u> and made an <u>incredible</u> <u>video</u>.

4 To get <u>images</u> like <u>these</u> the <u>team</u> used <u>drones</u>.

SPEAKING Talking about gadgets

7 ▶ **5.3** Listen to the conversation. Why does speaker B like his smartwatch?

A: Is that a smartwatch?

B: Yeah.

A: **How do you like it?**   How is it? / What do you think of it?

B: Oh, I love it. It looks cool and it's really **easy to use**.   user-friendly / practical

A: Yeah? What does it do?

B: Oh, **a lot of** things. For example, it can connect to   lots of / loads of
my smartphone and send me messages.

A: Great. **How much do they cost?**   How much are they? / What do they cost?

B: This one was $200. But the newer ones cost more.

8 Practise the conversation with a partner. Practise again using the words on the right.

9 Work in pairs. Choose one gadget that you know about. What do you like or dislike about it? Share your opinions.

I have a new tablet.

What do you think of it?

It's OK. It's really light, but it's not very easy to use.

5.2 What does it do?

WEARABLE TECHNOLOGY

Check out the latest wearable gadgets. Some are available now, and others you may use in the future.

Smart glasses
These allow you to record or watch video. They also add useful information to what you see.

Vibrating tattoo
A special substance makes your skin vibrate every time you get a message or call on your mobile phone.

Spray-on clothes
Just spray on your skin and let it dry. You have real clothing!

Smart bracelet
The smart bracelet can change colour when your friends are nearby. It also lets you know when you get a message on your phone.

Gaming vest
Ouch! Wear it while you play computer games. You feel what it's like when someone hits you.

GRAMMAR *much, many, a lot of*

1 ▶ 5.4 Look at the infographic. Which of the gadgets would you like to wear?

2 ▶ 5.5 Listen to two people talking about wearable technology. Complete the sentences.

   1 The woman would like smart glasses to _____ .

   2 The man likes the fitness band because it tells him how far he _____ .

3 Read the sentences in the Grammar box. Complete the table with *much*, *many* and *a lot of*. Each option can be used more than once.

4 Read the sentences. Are they correct? Put a ✓ or X. Change the incorrect sentences so they are correct.

   1 I don't have many money to buy new technology.

   2 Wearable technology can help a lot older people.

   3 How many people in the world have smart glasses?

   4 These gadgets come with a lot of instructions.

   5 I don't take much photos.

   6 How many extra information do smart glasses give us?

MUCH, MANY, A LOT OF

How much wearable technology is really useful?

I take **a lot of** photos.

Do you use **a lot of** technology?

I do**n't** use **much** technology.

How many kilometres do you usually do?

Not many – about six on a good day.

	with countable nouns	with uncountable nouns
affirmative		
negative		
question		

Check your answers on page 141 and do Exercises 1–2.

LANGUAGE FOCUS Describing things and how they work

5 ▶ **5.6** Study the examples in the Language focus box.

DESCRIBING THINGS AND HOW THEY WORK

What **does** your smartwatch **do**?	It **can** connect to my smartphone. play music.
What **do** you **use** it **for**?	I **use** it **to pay** for things. **to track** my heart rate.
How many apps do you have on your smartphone?	Quite **a lot**. **Not many**. It's new. Only **a few** at the moment.
How much battery life does it have?	Quite **a lot**. I only recharge it at night. **Not much**. I charge it twice a day. Only **a little**. I need to recharge it every few hours.

For more information and practice, go to page 141.

6 Complete the sentences. Use your own ideas.

1 You can use a fitness band
to see how far you walk .

2 You can use a personal drone
.

3 You can use a smartwatch
.

4 You can use an e-reader
.

5 You can use a smart TV
.

7 ▶ **5.7** Complete the information. Circle the correct words. Listen and check your answers.

Hoverboards are not just for science fiction films. [1] *A few / much* companies now make these boards, which fly just [2] *a few / a little* centimetres above the ground.

Unfortunately, hoverboards only work on a special surface, so there are not [3] *many / much* places you can use them. They're also difficult to use – even pro skaters need [4] *many / a lot of* practice. And they also cost [5] *a lot of / much* money. Still, even at $10,000 each, one company's hoverboards sold out quickly.

The Hendo hoverboard

Pronunciation Sentence stress with modifiers

8 ▶ **5.8** Underline the stressed word in each question and each answer.

1 A: Do you have many apps?
B: Only a few.

2 A: How much battery life does it have?
B: Not much.

3 A: How often do you use it?
B: I use it a lot.

SPEAKING Wearable technology

9 Work in a group. Choose one of these items. Discuss how to make it into wearable technology. Think about the questions below.

a hat	trainers	a ring

- What is the gadget's name?
- What does it do?
- How does it work?

10 Join another group. Share your ideas.

I'd like to tell you about the Smart Ring.

OK. What does it do?

Well, it can connect to my smartphone and it changes colour when I get a text message.

5.3 Man or machine?

READING Flying like a bird

1 Work in pairs. Look at the photo. Discuss the questions.

   1 How do you think Yves Rossy controls his aircraft?

   2 How do you think he stays safe when he's flying?

2 ▶ **5.9** Read the article. Check your predictions.

FLYING LIKE A BIRD

A man stands at the open door of a helicopter, around 2,000 metres above the ground. On his back is a jet-powered wing. He starts his four **engines** and then jumps from the helicopter,
5 diving towards the ground at great speed. The man [1]arches his back to stop the dive, and now he's flying! This is not a scene from an action movie – it's just another day for the Jetman, Yves Rossy.

'I really have the feeling of being a bird', says
10 Rossy. He has little **equipment** and no controls to help **steer** the wing. He changes his direction simply by moving his body. 'It's really pure flying. It's not steering, it's flight.' He only has two [2]instruments – one to tell him the current height
15 and another to tell him how much **fuel** he has.

It's a different world from Rossy's previous career as an airline pilot – but safety is still important. If something goes wrong, Rossy has two parachutes for himself and another for his wing. If one engine stops, he can continue on 20 three or even two. 'So, plan B, always a plan B', explains Rossy.

After just less than ten minutes, the fuel is almost empty. Rossy opens his **parachute**, and he begins to fall gently to the ground. 25 Another successful flight is complete. In the future, Rossy hopes to make this kind of flight safer, and he says, 'I hope it will be for everybody'.

---

[1] **arch (v)** to bend into a U-shape   [2] **instrument (n)** a type of measuring device

Understanding a process

3 Look at the diagram. Number the sentences 1–4.

a He arches his back to stop the dive and starts to fly. _____

b He stands at the door of a helicopter or a plane and starts his engines. _____

c He opens his parachute and lands safely on the ground. _____

d He jumps and dives towards the ground. _____

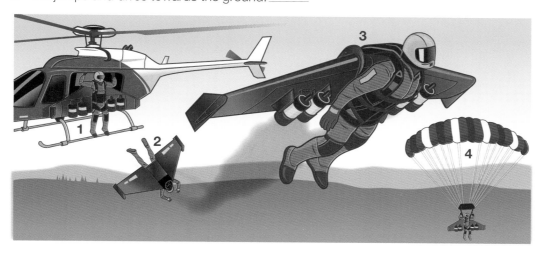

Understanding quotations

4 Circle the correct answers.

1 Why does Yves Rossy say, 'It's really pure flying'?

   a   because he controls his direction using only his body

   b   because his wings move up and down like a bird's wings

2 What does Rossy mean when he says, '... plan B, always a plan B'?

   a   He likes doing two things at the same time.

   b   It's important to prepare for possible problems.

3 What does Rossy mean when he says, 'I hope it will be for everybody'?

   a   He hopes everybody enjoys watching him fly.

   b   He hopes that everybody will be able to fly like him.

Understanding vocabulary

5 Complete the summary using the **bold** words from the article.

Yves Rossy doesn't need much [1]_____ when he flies. He uses his body
to [2]_____ and uses a [3]_____ when he lands. He carries
enough [4]_____ to fly for ten minutes. His [5]_____ give him
the speed to stay in the air.

6 Why do you think Yves Rossy has a parachute for his 'wing' as well as for himself?
Discuss with a partner.

5.4 Fly with the Jetman

TEDTALKS

1 Read the paragraph. Match each **bold** word to its meaning (1–4). You will hear these words in the TED Talk.

> **YVES ROSSY**'s idea worth spreading is that by using our bodies and technology together, we can have the amazing experience of 'pure' flying. In his unique **aircraft**, he can **climb** to an **altitude** of several thousand metres. He can also go fast – at one-third the **speed** of a passenger plane.

1 how fast something moves: _____

2 planes, helicopters, etc.: _____

3 height: _____

4 move upwards: _____

2 ▶ **5.10** Watch Part 1 of the TED Talk. What happens when Yves Rossy does these things (1–2)? Match. One option is extra.

1 He arches his back.

2 He pushes his shoulders forward.

a He flies up.

b He turns.

c He flies down.

3 ▶ **5.11** Watch Part 2 of the talk. Complete the notes.

What's his top speed?
About _____ km/h

What's flying like?
It's fun!
He feels like a _____ .

What's the weight of his equipment?
When his equipment is full of fuel, it weighs about _____ kg.

How did he become Jetman?
Rossy got the idea _____ years ago when he discovered free falling.

What's next for Jetman?
He wants to teach a _____ guy.
He wants to try taking off from a cliff.

CRITICAL THINKING

4 Yves Rossy hopes that his kind of flying 'will be for everybody' in the future. How does the technology need to improve for this to be possible? Discuss with a partner.

VOCABULARY IN CONTEXT

5 ▶ **5.12** Watch the clips from the TED Talk. Choose the correct meaning of the words.

6 Work in pairs. Discuss the questions.

1 Is there a language you would like to study instead of English?

2 In a plane do you feel safe when you take off and land?

PRESENTATION SKILLS Using gestures

TIPS

Gestures (movements with the hands) can be important when you present to a group. These tips can help you use gestures well.

- Keep your hands relaxed for most of the presentation.
- Make gestures large enough so your audience can see them.
- Use gestures to make words and ideas easier to understand.

7 ▶ **5.13** Watch the clip. Tick (✓) the things that Yves Rossy does.

He uses his hand(s) to show ...

a how big something is.

b the equipment behind him.

c how the harness goes around him.

d what flying is like.

8 Work in pairs. Read the extract from Chris Burkard's TED Talk. Discuss what kinds of gestures Burkard might make.

'There's only about a third of the Earth's oceans that are warm, and it's really just that thin band around the equator.'

9 ▶ **5.14** Watch the clip. What gestures does Chris Burkard actually make?

5.5 Great idea!

COMMUNICATE Inventing and selling a new app

1 Work in pairs. Think of some apps that you use or know about. Discuss what you like about them.

2 Think of an idea for a new app. What problem can it solve? How can it make life easier? Prepare a short description of the app to try to 'sell' the idea to a group of investors.

3 Take turns presenting your ideas to the class (the investors). Use gestures to help demonstrate how it works.

> **RESPONDING TO IDEAS**
>
> Good idea!
>
> That's a great idea!
>
> Interesting!
>
> Tell me more.

4 Take a class vote. Which app do you want to invest in?

WRITING Writing an online review

5 Read the review. What two pieces of information can you find about the Bussapp?

> ★ ★ ★ ☆ **Bussapp: Review**
>
> I often use this app for checking buses. It tells me the arrival time of the next bus and how many seats there are. It's very easy to use, but there is one thing I don't like …

6 Think about an item of technology you use or know about, such as an app, a gadget or video game. List several good points and bad points about it.

Good points	Bad points

7 Write a short review of the item from Exercise 6 to post online.

6 Challenges

Students take a high school exam in woods to help them relax, Henan province, China

WARM UP

Look at the photo and read the caption. Discuss the questions.

1 How do you think the students feel about taking an exam in a wood?

2 What do you think the advantages and disadvantages are?

3 What helps you relax when you face challenges?

In this unit you:

- talk about challenges
- describe sequence
- watch a TED Talk by **DANIEL KISH**

A waitress delivers food to customers in a busy restaurant in Memphis, United States

6.1 It's a big challenge

VOCABULARY Challenges

1 ▶ 6.1 Complete the challenges using these words. Listen and check your answers.

friends	health	money	pressure	stress

People sometimes think it's easy to be young, but students today face a lot of challenges. Many suffer from **exam** _____ – often caused by the need for good grades and _____ **from parents**. **Saving** _____ is also difficult when you're a full-time student. Some need to find part-time jobs to pay their tuition fees. And, as it becomes easier for students to study abroad, **making** _____ in a new country can also be difficult. What's more, all these kinds of worries can sometimes lead to serious _____ **problems**, such as depression.

Pronunciation /e/

2a ▶ 6.2 Listen to the words. Underline the /e/ sounds. Which two words don't have an /e/ sound?

1 money   3 health   5 pressure
2 stress   4 friends   6 challenge

2b ▶ 6.2 Listen again and repeat.

3 Work in pairs. Write the five challenges from Exercise 1 under the headings. Then add one more challenge for each heading. Share your information with another pair.

It's a big challenge for me	It's a challenge, but I can deal with it	It's not a problem for me

LISTENING It's no big deal

Listening for contrasts
There are certain words in English that speakers use to signal a contrast. Identifying these words is important for understanding a speaker's main message. Words that signal contrast include *but, however* and *although*.

4 ▶ **6.3** Listen to the information about Vasu Sojitra. Who taught him how to ski?

5 ▶ **6.3** Listen again. Circle the correct words.

1 Skiing *was / wasn't* the first sport Sojitra tried.

2 Skiing off-piste is a challenge because *the snow is thick / there are no ski lifts*.

3 Sojitra *likes / doesn't like* climbing the highest mountains.

4 Sojitra skis *at the same speed as / slower than* his skiing partners.

6 Do you know anyone who faces a similar challenge to Sojitra? Discuss with a partner.

Vasu Sojitra skiing in the United States

SPEAKING Talking about challenges

7 ▶ **6.4** Listen to the conversation. What is speaker B's challenge? What does speaker A suggest?

A: So, how do you like your new life here in Spain?

B: Well, it's a great place, but I'm feeling a bit homesick.

A: Oh, I **know how you feel**. I felt the same when I first moved here.
    know what you mean / understand

B: How did you **cope**?
    manage / deal with it

A: Well, when you move to a new country, it's really important to try hard to make some new friends. I **joined** a football team.
    started playing in / became a member of

B: That's a good idea. I like tennis. Maybe I can find a tennis club.

A: When you join a club, you meet people with similar interests.

B: Yeah, I guess you're right. Thanks for the **advice**.
    suggestion / help

8 Practise the conversation with a partner. Practise again using the words on the right.

9 Think of three challenges you face. Work in pairs. Share your challenges. Say what you do to face them.

I get a lot of pressure from my parents about my exam results.

Yeah, that's tough. How do you cope?

6.2 How do you cope?

GRAMMAR Time clauses

1 ▶ **6.5** Look at the infographic. Do you do any of these things to reduce stress? Discuss with a partner.

2 ▶ **6.6** Listen to two people talking about exam stress. What does the woman do to reduce her stress at exam time? Complete the sentences.

  1 Before the exam, she _____
_____ .

  2 After the exam, she _____
_____ .

3 Read the sentences in the Grammar box. Answer the questions (a–d).

4 Complete the sentences using the time clauses.

  1 I face any challenge / I try to think how to manage it

    Before _____ .

  2 I celebrate with my friends / I finish an exam

    After _____ .

  3 I feel stressed / My heart starts beating faster

    _____ when _____ .

  4 I usually ask for help / I don't know how to solve a problem

    When _____ .

  5 I take three deep breaths / I start any exam

    _____ before _____ .

  6 I finish a long day at work / I relax by playing video games

    After _____ .

TIME CLAUSES

I always listen to relaxing music **before** I have an exam.

After the exam, I reward myself by going shopping.

When I have an exam, I'm so stressed I can't think properly.

  a Time clauses can go *at the end / at the beginning / at either the beginning or the end* of the sentence.

  b What order do these events happen in: *do exam, listen to music, go shopping*?

  c Which word do we use when we mean two actions happen at the same time?

  d Which time clauses can be used as a preposition?

Check your answers on page 142 and do Exercise 1.

Pronunciation Linking with /r/

5a ▷ **6.7** Listen. Notice how the /r/ sound at the end of *before* and *after* is pronounced when the words are followed by a vowel sound.

After I finish an exam …

5b ▷ **6.8** Listen and repeat.

1 Before I start any exam …

2 After I finish a long day at work …

3 Before any challenge …

6 Complete the sentences with your own ideas. Compare with a partner.

1 Before I take a difficult exam,

_____ .

2 When I don't know the answer to an exam question, _____

_____ .

3 After I finish an exam,

_____ .

4 When I get my exam results,

_____ .

LANGUAGE FOCUS Describing sequence

7 ▷ **6.9** Study the examples in the Language focus box.

DESCRIBING SEQUENCE

When I get stressed, I go for a walk.

Before the exam starts, I look over my notes one last time.

After I finish the exam, I try not to think about it.

I feel more confident **when** I'm prepared for an exam.

I listen to relaxing music **before** I take an exam.

I always give myself a reward **after** I take my last exam.

Before you take an exam, you can do several things.

First, get a good night's sleep.

Then, have a light breakfast.

Next, try to get to school early.

After that, sit alone and relax.

For more information and practice, go to page 142.

8 ▷ **6.10** Complete the information. Circle the correct words. Listen and check your answers.

You are in the exam room waiting for your paper. Here are some tips to help you.

1 *First / Before* you start writing, read all the instructions carefully and slowly. Highlight any important details.

2 *Then / When*, check the back of the paper. Are there any more questions? Many people forget to do this.

3 When you're ready to start, answer the easy questions *first / next*.

4 *Before / When* you find a difficult question, don't spend too much time thinking about it. Move on to the next question and come back to it at the end.

5 *After / Before* you finish, don't leave the room early – check your answers carefully.

SPEAKING Dealing with exam stress

9 Work in pairs. You are going to teach each other some techniques for dealing with exam stress. Student A: Turn to page 150. Student B: Turn to page 153.

6.3 Living without fear

READING Seeing with the mind

1 Look at the lesson title and photo. What do you think the article is about?

    a how a blind man gets around   **b** why blind people have good hearing

2 ▷ **6.11** Read the article. Check your prediction.

SEEING WITH THE MIND

Everyone faces challenges in their life, but some are more significant than others. Daniel Kish was born with a type of eye ¹cancer and doctors **removed** both of his eyes before he was fourteen months old.

5 Soon after, however, he started to do an amazing thing. He started to make clicking sounds with his tongue to help him move around. Much like a ²bat, he now moves about using ³sonar. He is so good at it that he can ride a bicycle in traffic. He and his group, World Access for the Blind, teach
10 others how to use sonar. In this interview with *National Geographic*, Kish explains how the process works.

1 _____

'When I make a click sound, it makes ⁴sound waves. These waves **reflect** off surfaces all around and return to my
15 ears. My **brain** then processes the sounds into images. It's like having a conversation with the environment.'

2 **When you click, what do you see in your mind?**

'Each click is like a camera flash. I make a 3D image of my **surroundings** for hundreds of feet in every direction.'

20 **3** _____

'It's thrilling but requires a lot of **focus**. I click up to two times per second, much more than I usually do.'

4 **Is it dangerous to move around the world in this way?**

'Much of the world lives in fear of things that we mostly
25 imagine. I have a habit of climbing anything and everything, but I never broke a bone as a kid.'

5 _____

'Many students are surprised how quickly results come. Seeing isn't in the eyes; it's in the mind.'

---

¹ **cancer (n)** a serious disease where cells that are not normal spread to other parts of the body

² **bat (n)** a small animal that flies at night

³ **sonar (n)** a method for locating things by using sound waves

⁴ **sound waves (n)** movements in the air that carry sound to your ears

Understanding main ideas

3 Complete the article with these questions. Write **a**, **b** or **c** in the text.

    a How challenging is it to teach people to use sonar?

    b What is it like riding a bike using sonar?

    c How does human sonar work?

Understanding a process

4 How does flash sonar work? Look at the diagram. Number the sentences 1–5.

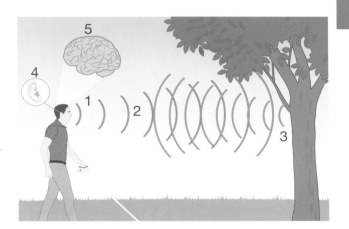

    a The sound waves reflect off surfaces. _____

    b The person makes a clicking sound. _____

    c The brain makes images with the sounds. _____

    d The sound waves reach the person's ears. _____

    e The sound waves travel away from the person. _____

Understanding details

5 Circle **T** for true or **F** for false.

    1 When Daniel Kish clicks, he can 'see' for more than a hundred feet.   **T**   **F**

    2 When Kish rides a bicycle, he clicks less than usual.   **T**   **F**

    3 As a child, Kish broke his arm when climbing a tree.   **T**   **F**

    4 Kish's students are usually surprised they can learn so fast.   **T**   **F**

Understanding vocabulary

6 Match the words in **bold** from the article to their definitions.

    1 remove   **a** special attention you give to something

    2 reflect   **b** to take away

    3 brain   **c** to send back light, sound, etc., from a surface

    4 surroundings   **d** the things around you

    5 focus (n)   **e** the part of you that controls your body and allows you to think

7 How easy do you think these things are for Daniel Kish to 'see' in his surroundings? Discuss with a partner.

    an open door   a road   a moving car   a tree

I think an open door is difficult for him to see because the sound waves won't reflect off it.

Yeah. You're probably right.

6.4 How I use sonar to navigate the world

TEDTALKS

1 Read the paragraph. Match each **bold** word to its meaning (1–4). You will hear these words in the TED Talk.

> **DANIEL KISH**'s **remarkable** solution to the challenge of 'seeing' for blind people has helped many people and **inspired** many others – even those who have not lost their sight. His idea worth spreading is that we all must **face** our challenges, and that we all have the ability to **navigate** these dark unknowns.

    1 to find a way: _____

    2 amazing: _____

    3 to try to overcome: _____

    4 made (somebody) want to do something: _____

2 What do you think 'these dark unknowns' refers to?

3 ▶ 6.12 Work in pairs. Read the extract from Daniel Kish's TED Talk and try to guess the missing words. Watch Part 1 of the TED Talk to check your guesses.

'Many of you may have heard me _____ as I came onto the stage … . Those are flashes of sound that go out and _____ from surfaces all around me, just like a _____'s sonar, and return to me with patterns, with pieces of information … . And my brain, thanks to my parents, has been activated to form images … .'

4 ▶ 6.13 Watch Part 2 of the TED Talk. Why does Daniel Kish say that he is not 'remarkable'?

    a because he has received a lot of help throughout his life

    b because everyone has to overcome challenges using their mind

5 ▶ 6.14 Watch Part 3 of the TED Talk. Put the events in the correct order (1–5) to describe the challenge Daniel Kish gives to the audience.

    a He makes a 'shhh' sound and moves the panel to show how the sound changes. _____

    b He holds the panel in front of his face and makes a 'shhh' sound. _____

    c He asks the audience to listen again and say 'now' when they hear the panel move. _____

    d Kish asks the audience to close their eyes. _____

    e The audience hears the panel move and says 'now'. _____

6 ▶ 6.15 Watch Part 4 of the TED Talk. Circle the correct options to complete the sentences.

    1 The video shows people who *can use flash sonar / find it terrifying to be blind*.

    2 Kish teaches flash sonar to *blind / blind and sighted* people from around the world.

CRITICAL THINKING

7 What are the similarities between the way Daniel Kish and Tom Thum use their voice? What are the differences? Discuss with a partner.

VOCABULARY IN CONTEXT

8 ▶ 6.16 Watch the clips from the TED Talk. Choose the correct meaning of the words.

9 Work in pairs. Complete the sentences in your own words.

    1 I'm terrified of …

    2 It takes me a while to …

PRESENTATION SKILLS Involving your audience

TIPS

When giving a presentation, it's important to keep your audience interested. One way of doing this is to involve them in your presentation. For example, you can:

- ask the audience to participate in an activity.
- teach them how to do something.
- find out about the audience.
- ask and/or answer questions.

10 ▶ 6.17 Watch the clip. Which of these things does Daniel Kish do to involve the audience?

    a He asks the audience to raise their hands.

    b He teaches the audience something.

    c He asks the audience to say a word.

11 ▶ 6.18 Watch the clip of Daniel Kish teaching the audience to see with sonar. Then work with a partner and try it. Close your eyes and use your textbook.

6.5 How do you deal with this?

COMMUNICATE Making suggestions

1 Work in a group. Choose one of these challenges or think of your own. Think about what someone might do to face the challenge. Make a list of at least six tips.

- making friends
- getting good marks
- finding a good job
- saving money
- health problems

INVITING OPINIONS

What do you think?
What's your opinion?
Do you agree?

2 Now create a poster with your information. Decide what visuals to include. How else can you make your poster interesting? Look at the infographic on page 64 for ideas.

3 Present your poster to the class. Make sure everyone in the group presents part of the poster. Try to involve your audience as much as possible.

WRITING Posting a challenge online

4 Read the blog post. What challenge does the post suggest?

Doing a 30-day challenge

Why not walk 10,000 steps every day for 30 days? First, get an app on your phone to count your steps. Next, decide where and what time of day you want to walk. After that, start walking!

5 Write a blog post. Suggest a 30-day challenge people can do. Suggest how to start using *first*, *next* and *after that*.

MODEL PRESENTATION

1 Read the transcript of Mark's presentation. Complete the text with these words.

after	expensive	health	many	play	talk
fun	heavy	much	quickly	tell	watch

I'd like to ¹_____ to you about a new piece of technology – a virtual reality headset. How many of you have one? Not so many. Well, I bought mine around a month ago, and I use it quite a lot.

First, I'd like to ²_____ you about the good points. I use it mainly to ³_____ video games. It makes the games much more ⁴_____. It feels very realistic, and it's amazing when you first try it. I also use it to ⁵_____ films, which is really cool.

There are some bad points, though. I'm not sure if it's good for my ⁶_____ or not. Sometimes, ⁷_____ I use it for a long time, I feel a little dizzy for a while. It's also quite ⁸_____, so it's a little uncomfortable to wear for a long time. It was ⁹_____ too – nearly $500 – and there aren't ¹⁰_____ games for it right now.

So, would I recommend it? I'd say no, not yet. I think it's best to wait for the price to come down and for the technology to improve. But I think this will happen very ¹¹_____.

Thank you very ¹²_____.

2 ▶ **P.2** Watch the presentation and check your answers.

3 ▶ **P.2** Review the list of presentation skills from units 1–6. Which does the speaker use? Tick (✓) them as you watch again.

Presentation skills: units 1–6			
The speaker:			
• introduces himself/herself	☐	• uses gestures well	☐
• uses good body language	☐	• involves the audience	☐
• introduces his topic	☐	• thanks the audience	☐

YOUR TURN!

4 Plan a short presentation to introduce a new piece of technology. It could be an app, a gadget or a video game. Use some or all of the questions below to make some notes.

- What is it?
- What does it do?
- How does it work?
- What are the good points about it?
- What are the bad points about it?
- Would you recommend it to others? Why? / Why not?

5 Look at the Useful phrases box. Think about which ones you will need in your presentation.

USEFUL PHRASES

Describing how something works

It can … / Using it, I can … / I can use it to …
It has a lot of … / It doesn't have much/many …

Positive words to describe gadgets

modern, easy to use, fast, light, strong, fun, cheap

Describing sequence

When/After I use it, I …
To use it, first you need to …
Then, …

Negative words to describe gadgets

old-fashioned, difficult to use, slow, heavy, weak, boring, expensive

6 Work in pairs. Take turns giving your presentation using your notes. Use some of the presentation skills from units 1–6. As you listen, tick (✓) each skill your partner uses.

Presentation skills: units 1–6

The speaker:
- introduces himself / herself ☐
- uses good body language ☐
- introduces his topic ☐
- uses gestures well ☐
- involves the audience ☐
- thanks the audience ☐

7 Give your partner some feedback on their talk. Include two things you liked, and one thing he or she can improve.

> That was great. Your body language was good, and you involved the audience. But you forgot to introduce yourself at the start.

7 Wild places

National Geographic Explorer
Andrés Ruzo studies the Boiling
River of the Amazon, Peru

WARM UP

Look at the photo and read the caption. Discuss
the questions.

1 What do you think the explorer in this photo
hopes to learn?

2 Do you think it's important to protect wild places?

3 Would you like to travel somewhere wild like this?
Where?

In this unit you:

- talk about the natural world
- make comparisons
- watch a TED Talk by **KAREN BASS**

Patagonia's Paine massif mountains rise beyond Lake Pehoé, Chile

7.1 The natural world

VOCABULARY Natural features

1 Look at these words. Which of these natural features can you see in the photo above? Which do you have in your country? Discuss with a partner.

beach	desert	lake	sea
canyon	island	mountain	waterfall

2 ▶ **7.1** Complete the sentences with these words. One word is extra. Listen and check your answers.

deep	dry	high	long	wide

1 China's Yangtze River is very _____ . It flows for 6,300 kilometres.

2 Mont Blanc is a very _____ mountain in Europe. It's 4,809 metres above sea level.

3 Russia's Lake Baikal is extremely _____ . Its bottom is 1,285 metres below sea level.

4 The Mississippi River in the United States is so _____ that you can't see across it in some places.

3 Look at the natural features in Exercise 1. Can you name any other examples? Why are they famous? Discuss with a partner.

There's Ninety Mile Beach in Australia. It's really long.

Yes, and there's the Grand Canyon in the United States. It's very deep.

74

LISTENING An amazing place

> **Listening for content words**
> Content words – such as main verbs, nouns and adjectives – carry the main meaning of a sentence. In spoken English, these words are usually stressed. Focusing on content words can help you understand the speaker's main message.

Marty Schnure and Ross Donihue in Patagonia

4 ▶ **7.2** Listen to the information about Ross Donihue and Marty Schnure's work in Patagonia. What did their work involve? Tick (✓) the correct option.

  a studying wildlife   **b** making a map   **c** collecting plants

5 ▶ **7.2** Listen again. Complete the sentences. Circle the correct words.

1 Patagonia is an area shared by *two / three* countries.

2 Patagonia is usually a very cool and *wet / dry* place.

3 Ross Donihue's favourite thing about Patagonia is *the changing conditions / the wildlife*.

Pronunciation Weak forms (2): The schwa /ə/ sound

6a ▶ **7.3** Listen to the weak forms in these sentences.

1 Patagonia is an area at the southern end of South America.

2 It's a big place but only about two million people live there.

6b ▶ **7.3** Listen again. Practise saying the sentences.

SPEAKING Talking about places

7 ▶ **7.4** Listen to the conversation. What is speaker A's favourite island?

A: So where are you going on holiday this summer?

B: Hawaii. **I'm really looking forward to it**!   **I can't wait / I'm really excited**

A: That's great! I know it well.

B: Really? I can't decide which island to visit – Oahu or Maui. I hear that Maui is **more relaxing**.   **quieter / more peaceful**

A: Yeah, maybe. But Oahu is more exciting. That's where Honolulu and Waikiki Beach are.

B: So would you say Oahu is the **best** place in Hawaii?   **nicest / most interesting**

A: No. Actually, my favourite island is Kauai. It's definitely the **most beautiful**. It has mountains, canyons, waterfalls and beaches. I love it there.   **prettiest / most scenic**

8 Practise the conversation with a partner. Practise again using the words on the right.

9 List three places in the world you'd like to visit. Explain your ideas to a partner.

> I'd love to go to the Grand Canyon. I'd like to hike to the bottom.

> Yeah, that sounds great. Me too.

7.2 It's the highest in the world

SEVEN WONDERS of the NATURAL WORLD

Our planet is home to some incredible natural wonders. Here are seven of the most amazing.

The best place to see the **Aurora Borealis** is northwest Canada.

Mount Everest is the highest mountain in the world.

Mexico's **Copper Canyon** is deeper and longer than the Grand Canyon.

Africa's **Victoria Falls** is the world's largest waterfall.

Other volcanoes may be larger than Mexico's **Paricutin Volcano**, but few are more beautiful.

The Great Barrier Reef is the world's largest coral reef system.

Rio de Janeiro's **harbour** is one of the most beautiful harbours in the world.

GRAMMAR Comparatives and superlatives

1 ▶ **7.5** Look at the infographic. Do you agree with the list of wonders?

2 ▶ **7.6** Listen to two people talking about the natural wonders. Complete the sentences.

1 The man thinks Paricutin Volcano is the _____ volcano in the world.

2 The woman says Copper Canyon is _____ than the Grand Canyon.

3 Read the sentences in the Grammar box. Choose the correct options to complete a–e.

4 Complete the sentences with the comparative or superlative forms of the adjectives.

1 Almeria in the south of Spain is the _____ city in Europe. (dry)

2 The Nile is _____ than the Amazon but the Amazon is _____ river in the world. (long, wide)

3 Some people say Mauna Kea in Hawaii is _____ than Mount Everest, but nearly 6,000 metres are under water. (high)

4 The mosquito is probably the _____ animal in the world. (dangerous)

5 I think the landscape near where I live is _____ than any other place I know! (beautiful)

COMPARATIVES AND SUPERLATIVES

Comparatives

I heard the Copper Canyon in Mexico is **more beautiful than** the Grand Canyon.

And here it says that it's **longer** and **deeper** too.

a Add -er / -est to short adjectives to make a comparative.

b Use more / the most before longer adjectives to make a comparative.

c Use that / than in comparatives that talk about two things.

Superlatives

They say it's **the most dangerous** mountain to climb.

That would be **the coolest** trip.

d Use the + -er / -est with short adjectives to make a superlative.

e Use more / the most before longer adjectives to make a superlative.

Check your answers on page 143 and do Exercises 1–2.

LANGUAGE FOCUS Making comparisons

5 ▶ **7.7** Study the examples in the Language focus box.

MAKING COMPARISONS

Comparing two things

Spring is a **better** time to visit **than** summer.
The problem with mosquitoes is **worse than** a few
years ago.
It's **further** to the sea **than** to the mountains
from here.

Is the Amazon **longer than** the Nile?
No, it isn't.
Which is **wider** – the Nile or the Amazon?
The Amazon (is **wider**).

Comparing three or more things

April is **the best** time to go there.
The mosquitoes here are **the worst** in
the world.
Where I live is **the furthest** you can be from
the sea.

Is the Nile **the longest** river in the world?
Yes, it is.
What's **the widest** river in the world?
The Amazon (is **the widest**).

For more information and practice, go to page 143.

6 Complete the sentences. Circle the correct words.

1 Let's go to Sydney in December. The weather
is *better than / the best* in June.

2 To me, summer is *worse than / the worst* time
to visit Jeju Island because of the crowds.

3 I would love to see Iguazu Falls in South America
one day. They look *really / more* beautiful.

4 Aconcagua is the second highest mountain
of / in the world.

5 The Thai islands all look interesting to me, but
Phuket sounds *better / the best*.

7 ▶ **7.8** Complete the text with the correct form of
the adjectives. Remember you may have to add
words. Listen and check your answers.

Mount Fuji is a symbol of Japan. At 3,776
metres, it is ¹_____ (high)
mountain in Japan. It is only 100 kilometres from
Tokyo, ²_____ (large) city in the
country.

Mount Fuji is ³_____ (popular)
tourist attraction in Japan. More than 200,000
people climb to the top every year. Climbing in
the summer is ⁴_____ (easy)
than in the winter. Few climb during the winter
as the conditions make it ⁵_____
(dangerous) than usual.

Many people start to climb Mount Fuji at
night. ⁶_____ (good) place to
experience sunrise is from the top. Japan, after
all, is nicknamed the 'Land of the Rising Sun'.

Pronunciation Stressed and weak syllables

8a ▶ **7.9** Listen to the <u>stressed</u> and *weak* syllables
in this sentence. Then listen again and repeat.

Is C<u>a</u>n<u>a</u>da <u>bi</u>gger th<u>a</u>n the <u>States</u>?

8b ▶ **7.10** Listen to these sentences. Underline
the stressed syllables. Listen again and
circle the weak syllables. Practise saying the
sentences.

1 Spring is a better time to visit than summer.

2 Is the Amazon longer than the Nile?

3 Mount Everest is higher than K2.

SPEAKING What do you know?

9 What do you know about some of the world's
natural wonders? Student A: Turn to page 153.
Student B: Turn to page 150. Do the quiz.

10 Work in pairs. Write three quiz questions
of your own. Then ask another pair your
questions. (Be sure you know the answers!)

What's the largest continent in the world?

Is it Asia?

7.3 An otherworldly place

READING Life in the Altiplano

1 Look at the photo and read the first paragraph of the article. Do you think the statements below are true (T) or false (F)? Discuss with a partner.

1 The Altiplano is a very high place.   **T**   **F**

2 The Altiplano is in Africa.   **T**   **F**

3 Very few people live in the Altiplano.   **T**   **F**

2 Read the article quickly to check your guesses.

LIFE IN THE ALTIPLANO

In the high Andes of South America lies one of the most incredible landscapes in the world. The Altiplano, or 'high plain', is a place of [1]extremes.

It is the second-largest mountain **plateau** in the world. It holds the world's largest high-altitude lake, Lake Titicaca, and the largest [2]salt flat, Salar de Uyuni. At 4,500 metres, it is also higher than many of the world's mountains.

Most of the Altiplano lies within Bolivia and Peru, while its southern parts lie in Chile and Argentina. The Atacama Desert – one of the driest areas on the planet – lies to the south-west. The Amazon rainforest lies to the west.

It is an [3]otherworldly **landscape** that looks more like Mars than Earth. High volcanoes **contrast** with deep valleys. Temperatures can change from boiling hot to freezing cold in a single day. Few trees can survive the dry conditions.

But suprisingly, animal life [4]thrives here. There are mammals, such as llamas, foxes and alpacas. There are also birds like the high-flying condors and three **species** of South American flamingos. Millions of people live in the Altiplano, too; most live in the area between Lake Titicaca and Salar de Uyuni. In fact, this is where Bolivia's most **populated** city, La Paz, is.

---

[1] **extremes (n)** conditions much colder, hotter, drier, etc., than the usual

[2] **salt flat (n)** a level area of land covered in salt

[3] **otherworldy (adj)** strange, as if from another planet

[4] **thrive (v)** to do well and be successful

Understanding main ideas

3 ▶ **7.11** Read the article. Choose the best alternative title.

    a South America's natural wonders

    b Land of extremes

    c Animals at high altitude

    d The highest city in the world

Understanding details

4 Read the article again. Complete the notes.

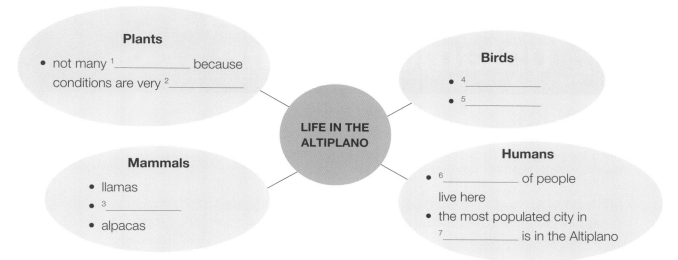

Plants
- not many ¹_____ because conditions are very ²_____

Mammals
- llamas
- ³_____
- alpacas

LIFE IN THE ALTIPLANO

Birds
- ⁴_____
- ⁵_____

Humans
- ⁶_____ of people live here
- the most populated city in ⁷_____ is in the Altiplano

5 Match each place (1–4) to the phrase that describes it.

    1 La Paz

    2 The Atacama Desert

    3 Lake Titicaca

    4 Salar de Uyuni

    a the largest high-altitude lake in the world

    b the largest salt flat in the world

    c one of the driest areas in the world

    d the most populated city in the Altiplano

Understanding vocabulary

6 Complete the definitions with a **bold** word from the article.

    1 A _____ is a large area of high, flat land.

    2 A _____ is everything you see when you look at an area of land.

    3 A _____ is a group of animals or plants with the same characteristics.

7 Choose the correct options to complete the definitions.

    1 If a place is **populated**, people *live / don't live* there.

    2 If two things **contrast**, they are *the same / different*.

8 Are there any incredible landscapes in your country? What kinds of animal species live there? Discuss with a partner.

7.4 Unseen footage, untamed nature

TEDTALKS

1 Read the paragraph. Choose the correct options to complete the definitions (1–4). You will hear these words in the TED Talk.

> **KAREN BASS**'s idea worth spreading is that world travel and new technology have allowed her to see and **capture** on film some **wonderful** and **brand new** things in nature and share them with millions of people. Karen Bass shows that when you have a job you love, even long hours and **tough**, challenging situations can't affect your passion for your work.

    1 If you **capture** something on film, you *record / erase* it.

    2 Something that is **wonderful** is *great / sad*.

    3 Something that is **brand new** is *completely / often* new.

    4 A **tough** job is very *easy / difficult*.

2 ▶ **7.12** Watch Part 1 of the TED Talk. Choose the correct options to complete the sentences.

    1 New technology helps Karen Bass to _____ .

      a   get new images and talk about new things   b   share her videos with many more people

    2 Karen Bass says she is also excited when _____ .

      a   she travels to a new place   b   new animal species are discovered

3 ▶ **7.13** Watch Part 2 of the TED Talk. If human, how long would the bat's tongue be? Choose the correct diagram.

  a   **b**   **c**

4 ▶ **7.14** Watch Part 3 of the TED Talk. Choose the correct options.

1 Karen Bass says the Altiplano is:

a somewhere she loves to go back to   b the most beautiful place in the world

2 What does Bass say is an advantage of the Altiplano's thin atmosphere?

a Few people live there.   b It's easy to see stars.

CRITICAL THINKING

5 Which three of these four things does Karen Bass do to share her passion?

a gives reasons for why she loves her job   **c** shows beautiful images

b tells us a story about an experience   **d** brings a real example onto the stage

6 Work in pairs. Choose two ways from Exercise 5 to share a passion you have.

VOCABULARY IN CONTEXT

7 ▶ **7.15** Watch the clips from the TED Talk. Choose the correct meaning of the words.

8 Work in pairs. Discuss the questions.

1 Do you have a favourite TV series? Can you describe it?

2 What places do you like going back to? Do you have one favourite place you like visiting?

PRESENTATION SKILLS Showing enthusiasm

You can show you are enthusiastic through the language you use. Instead of using words like *good* or *nice*, you can use stronger adjectives such as:

amazing   brilliant   fantastic   wonderful

9 ▶ **7.16** Watch the clips from Karen Bass's TED Talk. Complete the sentences.

1 'There are so many _____ places. But some locations draw you back time and time again.'

2 'But the advantage of that _____ thin atmosphere is that it enables you to see the stars in the heavens with _____ clarity.'

3 'Thank you so much for letting me share some images of our _____, _____ Earth.'

10 Read the extract from a presentation. What words could you add to make the speaker sound more enthusiastic?

India is a nice place. There are so many things to do. You can visit the beaches in Goa, sail down the River Ganges, and of course, you have to see the Taj Mahal.

11 Work in pairs. Take turns reading the extract. Who sounds the most enthusiastic?

The night sky in the Altiplano

7.5 Our natural wonders

COMMUNICATE Choosing tourist attractions

1 Work in a group. Brainstorm a list of your country's natural attractions. Think about lakes, rivers, forests, parks, etc.

> We have some nice national parks. How about one of those?

> Good idea. I think Seacoast Park is the most beautiful park.

2 Which attractions would foreign visitors like the most? Agree on three.

EXPRESSING AGREEMENT			
I agree.	You're right.	That's a good point.	Good idea.

3 Create a poster for your attractions. Think about what you want to include and take notes. Include photos, pictures or diagrams to make it interesting.

- best time to visit
- what's special about it
- interesting facts
- how to get there
- what to see there
- what to do there

4 Hold a class poster session. Look at your classmates' posters and present your own. Remember to sound enthusiastic when you give your presentation.

WRITING Making a recommendation

5 Make notes on a place you know that you would like to recommend to others.

Place: _____

Location: _____

Best time to go: _____

Why visit?: _____

6 Write about the place. Make it sound as interesting as possible.

> I recommend visiting Whistler Mountain in British Columbia, Canada. You can visit any time, but for me the best time to visit is the winter. I love skiing and Whistler has really amazing skiing. It's a fantastic place!

8 Confidence

A woman dances on a summer afternoon, St Petersburg, Russia

WARM UP

Look at the photo and read the caption. Discuss the questions.

1 Why do you think the woman in the photo is dancing alone?

2 Would you feel confident dancing like this?

3 Do you prefer being part of a group or doing things alone?

In this unit you:

- talk about appearance and personality
- describe people
- watch a TED Talk by **MEAGHAN RAMSEY**

8.1 A friendly face

VOCABULARY Appearance and personality

1   Read the descriptions. Add the **bold** words to the correct column in the table.

❝ Hi. My name's Kyle. I'm seventeen years old and I'm quite **short** for my age. But people say I'm **handsome**. I agree! I have two close friends – Nate and Amanda. Nate is kind of **shy** and not very **talkative**. But he can be really **funny**. Amanda is **tall** and **thin**. Some people say she can be **selfish**, but I don't think so. ❞

Appearance		Personality	
attractive	overweight	easy-going	clever
beautiful	pretty	honest	unfriendly

2   Look at the words in Exercise 1. Which words have a positive meaning? Which have a negative meaning? Discuss with a partner. Are there any words that you don't agree on?

Pronunciation Word stress

3   ▶ 8.1 Listen to these words from Exercise 1. Put them in the correct column.

Oo	Ooo	oOo	ooO	ooOo
		attractive		

4   Look at the image on this page. Work in pairs. Talk about some of the people.

I think this person is really pretty.   Yeah. And she looks friendly.

LISTENING Like mother, like daughter

> **Listening for similarities**
> The following phrases are used to describe similarities.
>
> We're **both** short.   **Both of us** like eating out.
> **Neither of us** are very tall.   We look **the same**.

5 ▷ **8.2** Listen to Bonnie Kim talking about herself and her mother. Tick (✓) the words you hear.

a	talkative	**c**	easy-going	**e**	funny
b	shy	**d**	quiet	**f**	tall

6 ▷ **8.2** Listen again. Circle **T** for true or **F** for false.

1 Bonnie and her mother are both quite tall.   T   F

2 Bonnie is talkative, but her mother is very quiet.   T   F

3 Bonnie and her mother both like sports.   T   F

4 Bonnie and her mother both enjoy cooking.   T   F

7 In what ways are you similar to your parents? Discuss with a partner.

Bonnie Kim takes a selfie with her mother in Seoul, South Korea

SPEAKING Talking about family

8 ▷ **8.3** Listen to the conversation. How are speaker B and his father similar?

A: Wow, that's a great photo! Is that your dad?

B: Yeah.

A: You look **just** like him.   **exactly / a lot**

B: Do you think so?

A: Yeah, you have the same **nose**.   **eyes / mouth**

B: I guess so. But we have really different personalities.

A: Really? What's he like?

B: Well, he's really talkative but I'm **quite** quiet.   **a bit / fairly**

A: And I guess that's your mum. She looks really **nice**.   **happy / friendly**

B: Yeah, she is. Everyone loves my mum.

9 Practise the conversation with a partner. Practise again using the words on the right.

10 Write the names of four members of your family. Work in pairs. Ask each other about the people.

What's your sister like?

She's really easy-going and fun.

8.2 He's kind of shy

HOW HAPPY ARE YOU WITH THE WAY YOU LOOK?

Tens of thousands of people from around the world recently answered this question.
According to the results, Mexicans are the happiest with the way they look.

The 5 HAPPIEST countries

% of people who are happy with how they look

1. Mexico **74%**
2. Turkey **71%**
3. Ukraine **65%**
4. Brazil **65%**
5. Argentina **62%**

The 5 UNHAPPIEST countries

% of people who are unhappy with the way they look

1. Japan **38%**
2. United Kingdom **20%**
3. South Korea **19%**
4. Australia **19%**
5. Poland **17%**

GRAMMAR Modifying adverbs

1 ▶ 8.4 Look at the infographic. Is your country shown? If not, how do you think it compares?

2 ▶ 8.5 Listen to an expert talking about the survey. Complete the sentences. Circle the correct options.

   1 In the survey, responses from men and women were very *similar / different*.

   2 12% of both men and women said they were *extremely / fairly* happy with the way they look.

   3 14% of women said they were *not very happy / not happy at all* with the way they look.

3 Read the sentences in the Grammar box. Answer the questions (a and b).

Pronunciation Stress with modifying adverbs

4a ▶ 8.6 Listen and underline the stressed word in each sentence.

   1 She's extremely talkative.

   2 He's really handsome.

   3 They're quite funny.

   4 I'm not very tall.

   5 We're pretty easy-going.

4b ▶ 8.6 Listen again and repeat.

5 Write five sentences about yourself. Use modifying adverbs and five adjectives from Exercise 1 on page 84. Tell a partner.

I'm quite shy.

MODIFYING ADVERBS

What's also **really** interesting is …

12% of both men and women said they were **extremely** happy with the way they look.

14% of women said they were **not very** happy with their looks.

4% of women said they were **quite** unhappy …

a Which words in bold make the adjective stronger?

b Which words in bold make the adjective weaker?

Check your answers on page 144 and do Exercise 1.

LANGUAGE FOCUS Describing people

6 ▶ **8.7** Study the examples in the Language focus box.

DESCRIBING PEOPLE

What's she like?	She's	extremely very / really pretty quite	talkative. friendly. easy-going. shy.
What does he look like?	He's	kind of / sort of fairly a bit not very	short. thin. overweight. tall.

He thinks he's **too** short.

He thinks he's **not** tall **enough**.

For more information and practice, go to page 144.

7 Put the words in order to make sentences.

1 honest / not / is / Lucia / very
2 clever / pretty / Paul / is
3 is / of / short / Chris / kind
4 I / short / is / hair / my / too / think
5 thinks / enough / not / thin / Jack / he's

8 Match each sentence to the phrase with a similar meaning (a or b).

1 He's too young.   **a** not very old
2 He's pretty young.   **b** not old enough

3 He's really unfriendly. **a** extremely unfriendly
4 He's a bit unfriendly.   **b** a little unfriendly

5 He's kind of talkative. **a** really talkative
6 He's extremely talkative. **b** fairly talkative

9 ▶ **8.8** Complete the information. Circle the correct words. Listen and check your answers.

Poor body image is not just a problem for women. Many men are also ¹*fairly / enough* unhappy with the way they look – and experts believe the problem is getting worse. Like many women, some men believe that they are ²*a bit / not very* overweight. But many others believe that they are ³*enough / too* thin or not tall ⁴*enough / too*. As a result, there are more men these days who develop serious health problems because of their body image issues. What's also ⁵*very / too* worrying is that men who suffer with these problems often don't talk to anybody about it.

SPEAKING A film of your life

10 Imagine you are making a film about your life so far. Write the names of four important people in your life. These people will be the main characters in your film.

11 Now think about which actors you'd like to play the different characters. Think about their appearance, age and personality. Explain your choices to a partner.

I'd like Tom Cruise to play me. He's quite short and he's extremely handsome.

OK. But he's too old. You're only 22!

8.3 A healthy body image?

1 Read the first paragraph of the article. What problem is mentioned? What do you think causes this problem? Discuss with a partner.

2 ▶ 8.9 Read the article. What possible solutions are mentioned?

THE PRESSURE TO BE 'PERFECT'

1 Body image – the way people feel about their appearance – is a big **issue** for many young people today. According to two different studies, more than half the teenage girls in the United States think they should [1]be on a diet, and almost one in five teenage boys are worried about their bodies and their weight.

2 But what's the cause? Many blame [2]the media. Turn on the TV and you'll probably see beautiful models, handsome actors and fit sports stars. Open a magazine or newspaper, browse the Internet, and it's usually the same.

3 Many young people feel [3]pressure to look like these 'perfect' people. But for most, this is just not possible. In the USA, for example, the average woman is 163 centimetres tall and weighs 64 kilograms. The average model is 180 centimetres tall and weighs 53 kilograms.

4 When people don't look the way many famous people look, they may develop low **self-esteem**. Some stop eating **properly** in order to lose weight. Students can lose so much confidence that they start to **withdraw** from classroom activities at school.

5 Body image issues do not disappear as we get older, either. In the United Kingdom, for example, women over 50 spend more money on [4]cosmetics than any other age group. Older men spend large amounts of money trying to **avoid** hair loss.

6 Is there a solution to the problem? A 2013 study in the UK recommended that body image lessons should be provided in schools. Others believe it's a problem that all of society needs to tackle. As Meaghan Ramsey says, 'We need to start judging people by what they do, not what they look like.'

---

[1] **be on a diet (phrase)** eat only certain foods to lose weight
[2] **the media (n)** radio, newspapers, magazines, etc.
[3] **pressure (n)** the feeling that you must do something
[4] **cosmetics (n)** make-up (and creams, etc.) that people put on their face and body to look more attractive

Understanding main ideas

3 Read the article again. What is the main idea of each paragraph? Write the paragraph number next to the main idea (a–f).

a There is no simple answer. We all need to change the way we think. _____

b Body image problems also affect adults. _____

c Many people think they need to look the same as the people in the media. _____

d Many young people today are worried about their appearance. ___1___

e Some people think the media focuses too much on appearance. _____

f People can lose confidence if they compare themselves to the people in the media. _____

Understanding statistics

4 Are the following statements true or false, according to the information in the article? Circle **T** for true or **F** for false.

1 Most teenage girls in the US believe they should be on a diet. T F

2 More than half of teenage boys in the US are worried about their weight. T F

3 The average female model in the US is seventeen centimetres taller than the average woman. T F

4 In the UK, teenage girls spend more money on cosmetics than adults. T F

Understanding vocabulary

5 Choose the correct options to complete the definitions.

1 A big **issue** is an important _____ .
   a problem   b solution

2 If you have low **self-esteem,** you are _____ in yourself.
   a confident   b not confident

3 If you **withdraw** from something, you _____ it.
   a continue to do   b stop doing

4 If you do something **properly,** you do it _____ .
   a in a different way   b in the correct way

5 If you **avoid** hair loss, you do something to _____ .
   a stop it from happening   b make it happen

6 Do you think the media affects your self-esteem? If so, in what way? What might be some other reasons people have low self-esteem?

Yes, I think the media affects how I feel about my weight.

For me, it's not the media. Other people's opinions have a bigger effect on how I feel.

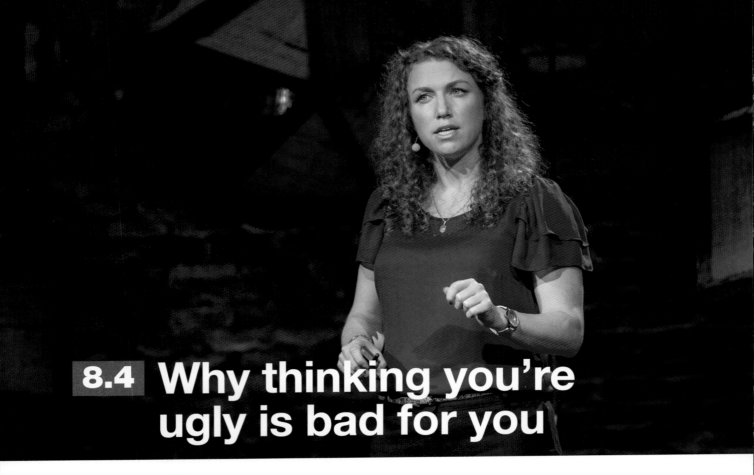

8.4 Why thinking you're ugly is bad for you

TEDTALKS

1 Read the paragraph. Match each **bold** word to its meaning (1–4). You will hear these words in the TED Talk.

> **MEAGHAN RAMSEY** feels we should **judge** people by what they do, not what they look like. She runs a global programme that is helping seventeen million young **individuals** improve their self-esteem by encouraging them to **value** their **whole** selves, not just their appearance. Her idea worth spreading is that changing the way we think about beauty can help our health and well-being and can improve society as a whole.

1 people: _____

2 to think something is important: _____

3 to develop an opinion about something: _____

4 all of something: _____

2 ▶ 8.10 Watch Part 1 of the TED Talk. Answer the questions.

1 Why is Faye worried about going to school?

a because she doesn't have any friends

b because people say that she's ugly

2 Why does Faye post a video of herself online?

a because her friends do the same thing

b so people can comment on her appearance

3 According to Meaghan Ramsey, why do many others post videos like Faye's?

a because online comments are really important to them   b because they feel alone

3 ▶ 8.11 Watch Part 2 of the TED Talk. Circle **T** for true or **F** for false.

1 Body image issues can affect a student's performance at school.   T   F

2 The problem is worse in the US than in other countries.   T   F

3 The main issue is how students think they look, not how they actually look.   T   F

4 ▶ 8.12 Watch Part 3 of the TED Talk. What suggestions does Meaghan Ramsey make about how to 'change our culture's obsession with image'? Tick (✓) all that apply.

   a Think carefully about the pictures and comments that we post on social networks.

   b Say more nice things about people's appearance to improve their confidence.

   c Stop letting young people use social networks during school.

   d Focus less on attractive people and more on those who make a difference in the world.

CRITICAL THINKING

5 Read the social media posts. How do you think Meaghan Ramsey would feel about each one? Discuss with a partner.

S	**Sandy**	Wow! You've lost a lot of weight. Well done!
D	**DD93**	Venus Williams is my favourite tennis player. She's so beautiful!
L	**Lukas**	Congratulations on your exam results!

VOCABULARY IN CONTEXT

6 ▶ 8.13 Watch the clips from the TED Talk. Choose the correct meaning of the words.

7 Work in pairs. Discuss the questions.

   1 What do you do to get ready to go out in the morning?

   2 Are you always available on social media and on your mobile phone? Why? / Why not?

PRESENTATION SKILLS Using statistics

TIPS

You can use statistics to support any claims you make in a presentation.

Nine out of ten people …   **Five per cent** of students …
One in three women …   Every day, **500** men …

8 ▶ 8.14 Watch the clips. Complete the sentences with the numbers you hear.

   1 '_____ people every month google, "Am I ugly?"'

   2 '_____ out of _____ girls are now choosing not to do something because they don't think they look good enough.'

   3 '_____ per cent, nearly _____ in _____ teenagers, are withdrawing from classroom debate.'

   4 '_____ in _____ are not showing up to class at all on days when they don't feel good about it.'

9 Look at the sentences in Exercise 8. Which of the statistics do you find most surprising? Do you think the numbers are similar in your country? Discuss with a partner.

8.5 What do you think?

COMMUNICATE A class survey

1 Work in pairs. Discuss the questions. Explain your answers.

   1 Do you think the media in your country focuses too much on appearance?

   2 Do you think teenagers worry more than adults about their appearance?

   3 Do you think teenage girls have more body issues than boys?

   4 Is it OK to comment on a post that asks, 'Am I ugly?'?

   5 Do you think it's a good idea for schools to have body image lessons?

   6 Would you ever consider plastic surgery?

   7 Do you worry about the number of 'likes' you get on social media?

   8 Do you think beauty contests are a bad thing?

CHOOSING NOT TO ANSWER A QUESTION

If you don't want to answer a question, these are a few things you can reply.

| Sorry, I'd rather not say. | I'd prefer not to answer. | No comment! |

2 Work as a class. Ask the questions in Exercise 1. How many people answer 'yes'? How many answer 'no'? Make a note of the results.

	1	2	3	4	5	6	7	8
Yes								
No								

3 Work in pairs. Discuss the results of the class survey. Was anything surprising? Use statistics to describe the results.

> So, nine out of twenty people don't like beauty contests. That's less than half.

> Yeah. That's surprising! I thought it would be more.

WRITING Describing a friend

4 Read the description of Alfonso. Underline the appearance words and circle the personality words.

> I have a good friend called Alfonso. He's really clever and kind. He's also really tall and thin. We are in a lot of the same classes, so he often helps me study. He's pretty funny too. He sometimes …

5 Think of a good friend. What is he or she like? List four words that describe their personality and appearance.

6 Write a description of your friend. Use the notes from Exercise 5 to help you.

9 Achievement

Young farmers stand with their sheep after a competition, Anglesey, UK

WARM UP

Look at the photo and read the caption. Discuss the questions.

1 What do you think the children did to win this prize?

2 Can you remember a moment of achievement from your childhood?

3 How did you feel and why was it important to you?

In this unit you:

- describe personal achievements
- talk about the past
- watch a TED Talk by **ROBERT SWAN**

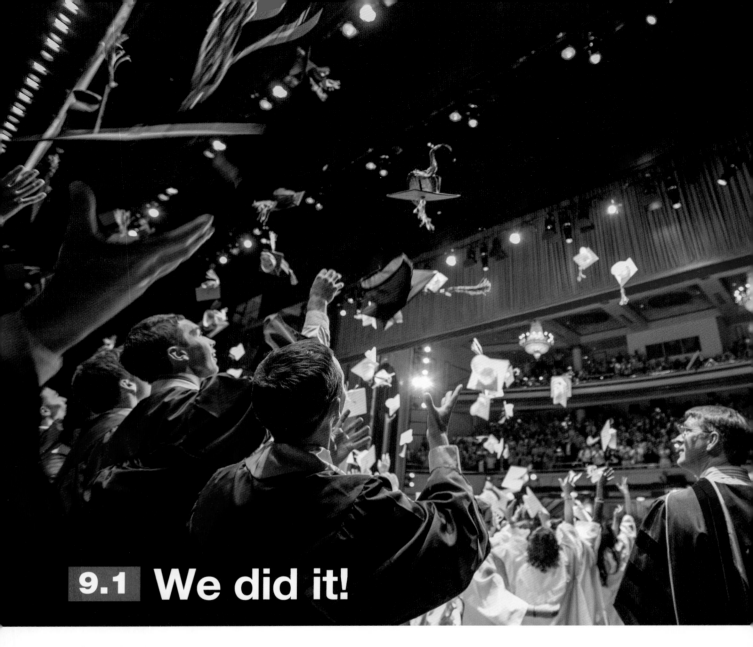

9.1 We did it!

VOCABULARY Personal achievements

1 Match the words in each set.

1	run	**a**	into shape	**7**	win	**a** a job
2	get	**b**	a new language	**8**	pass	**b** a competition
3	learn	**c**	a marathon	**9**	get	**c** an exam
4	climb	**a**	university	**10**	get	**a** a presentation
5	win	**b**	a mountain	**11**	give	**b** into university
6	finish	**c**	an award	**12**	start	**c** a business

2 Which of the achievements do you think are the most difficult? Why? Discuss with a partner.

Pronunciation Silent letters

3 ▶ **9.1** Listen to these words. Underline the silent letter in each word. Listen again and repeat.

1	climb	**3**	honest	**5**	scientist
2	island	**4**	friend		

LISTENING My great achievement

Listening for past tense expressions
Listening for certain time expressions helps you understand what time period a speaker is talking about. For example:

one year **ago**   **last** week   **When I was** a child, …

4 ▶ **9.2** Listen to Scott Leefe, a marathon runner. Tick (✓) his achievement.

a He ran twelve marathons in one year.

b He broke a national record for the marathon.

c He won a marathon in Iceland.

5 ▶ **9.2** Listen again. Match the events to the places.

1 Scott ran his first marathon in

2 His favourite marathon was in

3 His most difficult race was in

4 He finished in third place in

a Reykjavik, Iceland.

b Okinawa, Japan.

c Gwacheon, Korea.

d Kuala Lumpur, Malaysia.

Scott Leefe taking part in a marathon in Iceland

6 Do you know anyone who has achieved something similar to Scott Leefe? Discuss with a partner.

SPEAKING Talking about an achievement

7 ▶ **9.3** Listen to the conversation. What was speaker B's achievement?

A: How was the **race** last week?   **contest** / **competition**

B: Pretty good. I **came second**.

A: Oh, **well done**!   **congratulations** / **that's great**

B: Thanks! It **wasn't easy**.   **was hard** / **was tough**

A: Did you get a prize?

B: Yeah, I did. I won a £50 book voucher.

A: Great! You must be **really happy**.   **really pleased** / **delighted**

B: I am. It was really hard work, but it was worth it.

8 Practise the conversation with a partner. Practise again using the words on the right.

9 Think of something you achieved. Choose one of these ideas or think of your own. Join a group and talk about your achievement.

a time you won something

a time you learned something

a time you achieved a goal

a time you passed an important exam

9.2 Exploring the world

MILESTONES IN EXPLORATION

Edmund Hillary and Tenzing Norgay climbed Mount Everest.
1953

Neil Armstrong and Buzz Aldrin became the first people to walk on the moon.
1969

Robert Swan walked to the South Pole.
1986

Ann Bancroft and Liv Arnesen travelled across Antarctica.
2001

Gennady Padalka broke the record for the longest time spent in space.
2015

1963
Valentina Tereshkova became the first woman to travel to space.

1985
Robert Ballard discovered the *Titanic*.

1999
Bertrand Piccard and Brian Jones flew a balloon nonstop around the world.

2010
Sixteen-year-old Jessica Watson sailed alone around the world.

GRAMMAR Past simple

1 ▶ **9.4** Look at the infographic. Which achievement do you think is the most interesting?

2 ▶ **9.5** Listen to more information about Ann Bancroft and Liv Arnesen's achievement. Complete the sentences.

   1 Before they became explorers, Ann Bancroft and Liv Arnesen worked as _____.

   2 In 2001, they became the first women to cross the Antarctic on _____.

   3 Their journey across Antarctica took _____ months.

3 Read the sentences in the Grammar box. Answer the questions (a–c).

PAST SIMPLE

Ann Bancroft and Liv Arnesen **were** once school teachers.

They **became** the first women to cross the Antarctic on foot.

The journey **lasted** three months.

a Which verb in bold is a regular verb?

b Which verb in bold is the past of *to be*?

c Which verb in bold is another irregular past form?

Check your answers on page 145 and do Exercises 1–2.

4 Complete the facts about three explorers with these verbs.

arrived	discovered	got	sailed
tried	walked	was	wrote

Pytheas of Massalia, a Greek explorer, ¹_____ across the sea to Britain in about 325 BC. In his book, *On the ocean*, he ²_____ about the midnight sun in north-western Europe for the first time.

Many people believe **Leif Eriksson**, the Icelandic explorer, ³_____ North America 500 years before Columbus. In about 1000 BC, he ⁴_____ on his way to Greenland but the wind took him in the wrong direction. He ⁵_____ in a place he called Vinland – probably the north-eastern coast of the USA.

In the early 19th century, **Alexander von Humbolt** ⁶_____ around Latin America for five years. He and his team ⁷_____ to climb Chimborazo mountain in Ecuador. They didn't get to the top but they ⁸_____ higher than anyone else.

Pronunciation Regular past endings

5a ▶ **9.6** Listen to the pronunciation of these regular past forms.

/d/	/t/	/ɪd/
skied	walked	lasted

5b ▶ **9.7** Listen to these verbs and add them to the table in Exercise 5a.

1 climbed   **3** trained   **5** watched

2 finished   **4** visited   **6** completed

LANGUAGE FOCUS Talking about the past

6 ▶ **9.8** Study the examples in the Language focus box.

TALKING ABOUT THE PAST

Where **did** Piccard and Jones **begin** their balloon flight around the world?
They **began** in Switzerland.

How long **did** the journey **take**?
It took almost twenty days.

Were they successful?
Yes, they **were**.

Did they **make** any stops on their journey?
No, they **didn't**.

For more information and practice, go to page 145.

7 Look at the infographic on page 96. Write short answers to the questions.

1 Was Valentina Tereshkova the first woman in space?
Yes, she was.

2 Did Ann Bancroft and Liv Arnesen journey across the Arctic?

3 Did Edmund Hillary discover the *Titanic*?

4 Did Robert Swan walk to the South Pole?

5 Were Piccard and Jones the first people to walk on the moon?

8 ▶ **9.9** Complete the information with the correct form of the verbs. Listen and check your answers.

Sarah McNair-Landry ¹ <u>grew up</u> (grow up) in northern Canada. Her parents were Arctic guides, and she ² _____ (start) to explore from an early age. When she was eighteen, she ³ _____ (ski) to the South Pole. She ⁴ _____ (be) the youngest person ever to do this.

In 2007, McNair-Landry ⁵ _____ (decide) to snow-kite across Greenland. She ⁶ _____ (want) to raise awareness of global warming, and she ⁷ _____ (hope) to inspire a new generation of explorers.

In 2015, she and a friend ⁸ _____ (travel) for 120 days in the Arctic by dog sled. She ⁹ _____ (find) the most difficult thing about the trip was keeping the dogs happy. Often they simply ¹⁰ _____ (not want) to run.

Sarah McNair-Landry and her dog sled in the Arctic

9 Use the words to write questions. Ask and answer them with a partner.

1 you / pass / your last exam?
Did you pass your last exam?

2 when / you / last win / a prize?

3 what / you / achieve / last year?

4 be / you / a good student / at school?

SPEAKING Round-the-world adventure

10 You are going to read the story of Jessica Watson's round-the-world sailing trip.

Student A: Turn to page 152. Student B: Turn to page 149.

9.3 Arctic conditions

READING From Pole to Pole

1 Read the article quickly. What was Robert Swan's great achievement?

A photo of Robert Swan and a team member taken during the Antarctica expedition, 1985

FROM POLE TO POLE

1 From the age of eleven, Robert Swan knew he wanted to be an adventurer. Inspired by famous polar explorers Roald Amundsen and Robert Scott, Swan wanted to become the first person to
5 walk to both the North and South Poles. People told him he was crazy, but in 1985, after years of raising money, he began his adventure.

2 In January 1986, Swan and his team arrived at the South Pole after a 1,400-kilometre journey
10 through Antarctica's **extreme** conditions. Just three years later, Swan created a new team to **head** to the North Pole. After walking 1,000 kilometres in 60 days, the team arrived at its [1]destination. Swan, in his own words, became 'the
15 first person stupid enough to walk to both Poles'.

3 During those two [2]expeditions, however, Swan noticed some **frightening** things. At the South Pole, his eyes changed colour and his skin [3]blistered due to a hole in the [4]ozone layer. At the North Pole, 1,000 kilometres from safety, the ice   20 started to **melt beneath** his feet. This was four months earlier than the usual 'melt season'. These experiences made Swan realize something – the Poles were in real danger.

4 That feeling never left Swan. He now works to   25 [5]raise awareness about climate change and the ice melt of the South and North Poles. In doing this, Swan hopes that he can help not only in the preservation of these two amazing places, but also in our own **survival** here on Earth.   30

---

[1] **destination (n)** the place you're going to

[2] **expedition (n)** an organized trip for a special purpose

[3] **blister (v)** to develop painful swelling on the skin

[4] **ozone layer (n)** the part of Earth's atmosphere that protects us from the sun's ultraviolet rays

[5] **raise awareness (phrase)** make people understand

Understanding main ideas

2 ▶ **9.10** Read the article. Circle the main idea for each paragraph (1–4).

1 a From a young age, Swan wanted to explore the North and South Poles.

    b Swan was the youngest man to walk to the South Pole.

2 a The journey to the North Pole was more dangerous than the one to the South Pole.

    b In the 1980s, Swan became the first person to walk to both Poles.

3 a During the expeditions, Swan saw that the Poles were in danger.

    b Swan thought about stopping the expeditions due to the many dangers.

4 a Swan hopes that one day he can return to the South Pole.

    b These days, Swan works to teach people about the dangers of climate change.

Understanding details

3 Complete the Venn diagram with the information (a–h).

  a 1,000-kilometre journey

  b 1,400-kilometre journey

  c travelled with a team

  d arrived at his destination in 1986

  e arrived at his destination in 1989

  f ice started to melt four months earlier than usual

  g skin and eyes damaged due to hole in ozone layer

  h realized the Poles were in danger

Swan's expedition to the South Pole
_____
_____
_____

Swan's expedition to the North Pole
_____
_____
_____

Understanding vocabulary

4 Complete the paragraph. Use the correct form of the **bold** words in the article.

More than 100 years ago, Robert Falcon Scott [1]_____ to Antarctica in an attempt to become the first person to reach the South Pole. In January 1912, after a long and difficult expedition in the [2]_____ cold, Scott and his team successfully reached their destination. However, when they got there, they found they weren't the first! A Norwegian team, led by Roald Amundsen, had already arrived 34 days earlier. On the return journey, Scott's team faced a [3]_____ struggle for [4]_____ as they suffered in the intense cold. Sadly, Scott and his four companions all died before they reached home.

5 Complete the definitions. Circle the correct words.

  1 If something is **beneath** you, it is *above / below* you.

  2 An example of something that can **melt** is *ice cream / orange juice*.

6 What other places in the world have extreme conditions? Discuss with a partner.

9.4 Let's save the last pristine continent

TEDTALKS

1 Read the paragraph. Match each **bold** word to its meaning (1–4). You will hear these words in the TED Talk.

ROBERT SWAN has made it his **mission** to protect Antarctica. He knows from experience that what is happening there **threatens** the Earth's long-term health. His idea worth spreading is that the **preservation** of Antarctica is **linked** to our survival, and that it is possible for us to slow down the melting of ice at the South Pole.

1 connected: _____

2 a very important task: _____

3 to put in danger: _____

4 action of keeping the same: _____

2 ▶ **9.11** Watch Part 1 of the TED Talk. Circle **T** for true or **F** for false.

1 Robert Swan describes himself as an environmentalist.   **T   F**

2 On the expedition, Swan's team had radios so that they could call for help.   **T   F**

3 It was so cold that water could freeze in their eyes.   **T   F**

4 The journey to the South Pole took 90 days.   **T   F**

3 ▶ **9.12** Watch Part 2 of the TED Talk. Complete the summary with the numbers you hear.

Robert Swan has taken more than ¹_____ businesspeople and students to Antarctica so that they could experience the place for themselves. During these visits, they removed ²_____ tons of old waste metal over a period of ³_____ years and recycled it in South America. Swan has been to Antarctica ⁴_____ times. He believes everyone who goes there returns home as a champion* for this amazing place.

---
*champion (n) a supporter or defender of something

4 ▶ **9.13** Watch Part 3 of the TED Talk. What 'simple solution' does Robert Swan suggest to stop the melting of Antarctica's ice? Circle the correct answer.

a Use more renewable energy so people won't need to use Antarctica's resources. We may also slow down the melting of Antarctica's ice.

b Use renewable energy from Antarctica so people will realize how special the place is. It can also help slow down global warming.

CRITICAL THINKING

5 Robert Swan uses four stages of argument in his talk. Put them in the order he talks about them (1–4).

   a He describes his experience of taking lots of young people to Antarctica and starting to clean up the rubbish there. _____

   b He talks about using renewable energy to slow down the ice melt. _____

   c He describes his personal experience of being amazed, cold and frightened in Antarctica. _____

   d He gives information from NASA about how the ice in Antarctica is breaking up, but says there is a solution. _____

6 Which of these arguments has the biggest impact on you? Which makes you want to do something?

VOCABULARY IN CONTEXT

7 ▶ 9.14 Watch the clips from the TED Talk. Choose the correct meaning of the words.

8 Work in pairs. Complete the sentences in your own words.

   1 When I am on my own my favourite thing to do is ….

   2 One difficult thing I managed to do this year was …

PRESENTATION SKILLS Using pauses

TIPS

Pausing at an appropriate moment gives the audience time to stop and consider the speaker's message. You can pause after an important point or a question you want the audience to think about.

9 ▶ 9.15 Watch the clip. Notice how Robert Swan uses pauses when he speaks.

10 ▶ 9.16 Read the extract from the talk. Mark with a **/** where you think Robert Swan will pause. Watch and check your guesses.

   'I have faced head-on these places, and to walk across a melting ocean of ice is without doubt the most frightening thing that ever happened to me.'

11 Look at the paragraph about Robert Swan in Exercise 1. Imagine this is part of a presentation you are giving. Mark with a **/** where you think you should pause. Practise reading the paragraph in pairs.

A polar bear in the Arctic jumps from one piece of ice to the next

9.5 What's your claim to fame?

COMMUNICATE Discussing an achievement

1 Work in pairs. Think of a person who made an important achievement in one of these categories.

sports	medicine	education	exploration
entertainment	inventions	science	technology

2 Research information about the person. Find answers to some of these questions. Take notes.

What does this person do?

What was his or her achievement?

What did he or she need to do to achieve it?

What's your opinion of this person's achievement?

Did anyone help him or her?

Why is the achievement important?

How long did it take?

What other events in this person's life are important?

3 Use your notes to prepare to talk about the person and his or her achievement. Then tell another pair. Answer any questions.

INTERRUPTING POLITELY

Sorry, can I just stop you there?

Sorry, do you mind if I ask a question?

Sorry, can I just ask something?

WRITING Writing a biography

4 Read Usain Bolt's biography. What sport did he enjoy when he was a child?

5 Use your notes from Exercise 2 to write about a person who has achieved something important in his or her life. Include information about the person's background and childhood.

Usain Bolt was born in Jamaica in 1986. As a child, Bolt was interested in playing cricket, but his coach suggested that he should try running instead. Bolt took part in a 200-metre race at school and won with a time of 22.04 seconds.

Presentation 3 | UNITS 7–9

MODEL PRESENTATION

1 Complete the transcript of the presentation using these words.

ago	best	in	most	stayed	was
beach	didn't	largest	quite	too	were

I'd like to talk to you about the ¹_____ amazing place I've ever visited.

The Great Barrier Reef is the ²_____ coral reef system ³_____ the world. It stretches for more than 2,300 kilometres off the east coast of Australia. You can even see it from space!

I went there with my best friend about two years ⁴_____. We both really love diving, so this ⁵_____ our dream holiday. We ⁶_____ in a hotel on Heron Island, which is just off the coast. It's a beautiful place. The ⁷_____ thing about the island was that we ⁸_____ need to take a boat to visit the reef – the reef was right there, just off the ⁹_____.

We saw some amazing things while we were diving. There ¹⁰_____ so many different kinds of colourful fish. We even saw a sea snake that swam very close to us. To be honest, I was ¹¹_____ scared!

The only bad thing about my trip was that it was much ¹²_____ short. We stayed for three days and spent most of our time in the water. I'd love to go back again and maybe go diving in a different place.

Thanks for listening.

2 ▶ **P.3** Watch the presentation and check your answers.

3 ▶ **P.3** Review the list of presentation skills from units 1–9 below. Which does the speaker use? Tick (✓) them as you watch again.

Presentation skills: units 1–9
The speaker:
• introduces himself/herself ☐
• uses good body language ☐
• introduces his/her topic ☐
• uses gestures ☐
• involves the audience ☐
• uses statistics ☐
• shows enthusiasm ☐
• uses pauses ☐
• thanks the audience ☐

YOUR TURN!

4 Plan a short presentation about a place you've visited, or a place you'd like to visit. Use some or all of these questions to make notes.

- What's the name of the place?
- Where is it exactly?
- What's special about it?
- What did you do there? / What would you like to do there?

5 Look at the Useful phrases box. Think about which ones you will need in your presentation.

USEFUL PHRASES

Natural features:

beach, canyon, desert, island, lake, landscape, mountain, ocean, waterfall

Adjectives to describe natural features:

deep, dry, high, long, wide

Past time expressions:

ago, last, when I was …

Stronger adjectives:

amazing, brilliant, fantastic, incredible, magnificent, wonderful

6 Work in pairs. Take turns giving your presentation using your notes. Use some of the presentation skills from units 1–9. As you listen, tick (✓) each skill your partner uses.

Presentation skills: units 1–9

The speaker:

- introduces himself/herself ☐
- uses good body language ☐
- introduces his/her topic ☐
- uses gestures ☐
- involves the audience ☐
- uses statistics ☐
- shows enthusiasm ☐
- uses pauses ☐
- thanks the audience ☐

7 Give your partner some feedback on his or her talk. Try to include two things you liked, and one thing he or she can improve.

> That was great. You used pauses, and you showed enthusiasm. But you forgot to introduce your topic.

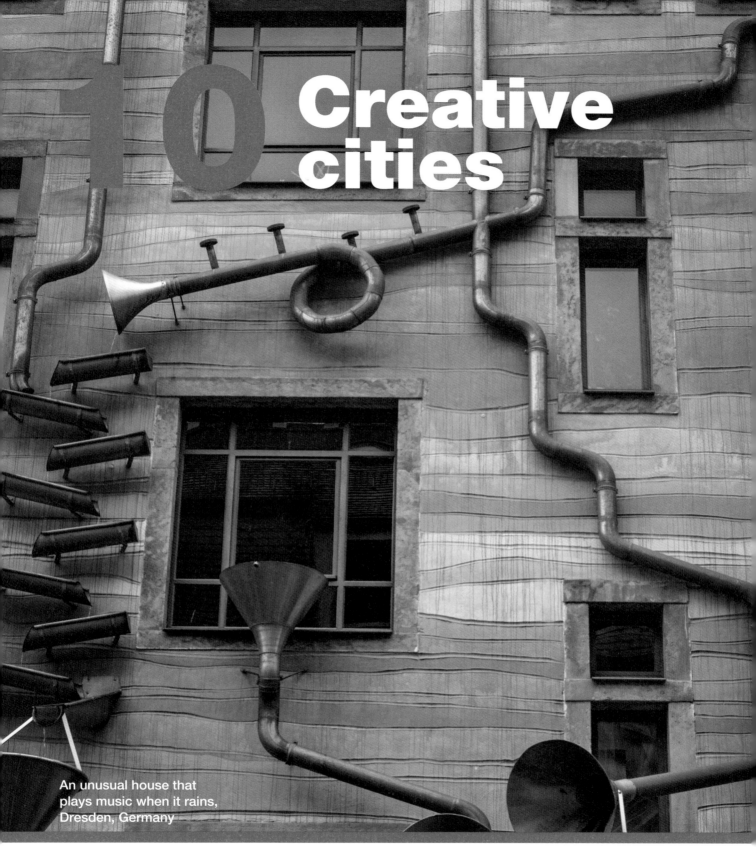

10 Creative cities

An unusual house that plays music when it rains, Dresden, Germany

WARM UP

Look at the photo and read the caption. Discuss the questions.

1 Why do you think someone decided to do this to their house?

2 Do you like this idea? Why? / Why not?

3 What other things do people do to make cities look more creative?

In this unit you:

- talk about a city
- make suggestions
- watch a TED Talk by **THEASTER GATES**

Young children playing
in the colourful streets of
Las Peñas, Ecuador

10.1 In the neighbourhood

VOCABULARY City life

1 Match the words in each set.

1 clean	**a** traffic		**5** low	**a** buildings
2 affordable	**b** streets		**6** green	**b** crime rate
3 heavy	**c** housing		**7** reliable	**c** space
4 friendly	**d** neighbours		**8** empty	**d** public transport

2 Which of the phrases in Exercise 1 describe positive qualities of a city or part of town? Which describe negative qualities? Compare with a partner. Are there any you disagree on?

3 Work in pairs. What other things do you think a good neighbourhood needs? What other problems do bad neighbourhoods have?

Pronunciation Combinations of consonants

4 ▶ **10.1** Listen to how two or more consonants sound together in a word. Listen again and repeat.

1 **cl**ean	**3** **fr**ien**dl**y	**5** **sp**ace
2 **st**ree**ts**	**4** **cr**ime	**6** **tr**an**sp**ort

LISTENING The place where I grew up

Identifying pros and cons
Taking notes using a table can help you understand the pros (good points) and cons (bad points) of something.

5 ▶ **10.2** Listen to Craig Albrightson talking about his hometown in South Africa. Circle the topics he mentions.

green space	crime	housing	traffic
nightlife	public transport	neighbours	jobs

6 ▶ **10.2** Listen again. Complete the table with words from Exercise 5. Add any extra details you hear.

Pros	Cons

A row of houses in Pietermaritzburg, South Africa

7 Does Craig Albrightson generally like or dislike his neighbourhood?

SPEAKING What's your neighbourhood like?

8 ▶ **10.3** Listen to the conversation. What doesn't speaker B like about her new neighbourhood?

A: I hear you moved to a new **place**.   **apartment / house**

B: Yeah, I did. I moved last month.

A: So how do you like your new area?

B: Well, it's OK. The streets are really clean and there are
a lot of **parks** nearby, but the traffic is really heavy.   **shops / restaurants**

A: Yeah? Maybe you should take the train.

B: I thought about it, but I heard it's not very reliable.

A: So **why don't you buy** a bike? It's good exercise.   **how about buying / why not buy**

B: Yeah, that's **a good idea**. I'll think about it.   **not a bad idea / a great idea**

9 Practise the conversation with a partner. Practise again using the words on the right.

10 Think about the area you live in. What are its pros and cons? Write notes. Work in pairs. Share what you like and don't like about your neighbourhood.

My area has a lot of nice shops. And the streets are really clean.

That's good. What don't you like about your area?

10.2 Nice neighbourhoods

WHAT MAKES A GREAT NEIGHBOURHOOD?

What do people look for when choosing a neighbourhood? A recent survey found that personal safety tops the list, but many other things also help.

- SAFETY AND LOW CRIME
- GREEN SPACE AND PARKS
- AIR QUALITY
- GOOD ROADS
- GOOD SCHOOLS
- AVAILABILITY OF JOBS
- ENTERTAINMENT AND NIGHTLIFE
- WATER QUALITY

GRAMMAR *should* and *shouldn't*

1 ▶ 10.4 Look at the infographic. Which things describe your neighbourhood?

2 ▶ 10.5 Listen to a couple talking about where to move. Tick (✓) the neighbourhoods that each person likes.

	Brentwood	Crestview	Woodlands
Man			
Woman			

3 Read the sentences in the Grammar box. Answer the questions (a and b).

4 Complete this advice, from Chinese feng shui, about the day you move house. Write *should* or *shouldn't*.

1 You _____ only say positive things. Don't say anything bad.

2 You _____ invite any guests – just family members!

3 You _____ buy new equipment to clean the house. Don't take the old things with you.

4 You _____ sleep in the afternoon. It suggests illness and laziness.

5 You _____ enter the house with nothing in your hand. Carry something that brings good luck, like fruit.

6 You _____ buy a gift for your house. It can be something big or small.

SHOULD AND SHOULDN'T

So, where **should** we move to?

We **shouldn't** leave it much longer.

Well, we **should** think about Woodlands.

a What form of the verb do we use after *should* and *shouldn't*?

b How do we form questions with *should*? Do we use *do*?

Check your answers on page 146 and do Exercise 1.

LANGUAGE FOCUS Making suggestions

5 ▶ **10.6** Study the examples in the Language focus box.

MAKING SUGGESTIONS

Let's
Maybe we/you can
We/You could   move house.
One thing we/you could do is

Why don't we/you move to a more central area?

How about moving somewhere cheaper?

What should I/we do?
You/We should live in Crestview.
You/We shouldn't move to Woodlands.

For more information and practice, go to page 146.

Pronunciation Positive intonation

6 ▶ **10.7** Listen to how we use intonation to make suggestions sound positive. Practise saying the sentences.

1 You could move to a smaller place.
2 Let's visit the local schools next week.
3 Why don't we try the bus service?
4 How about talking to some of the neighbours?

7 Match the sentence parts to make suggestions.

1 You should
2 Why don't you
3 How about
4 You shouldn't
5 Let's

a walk alone at night. It's not safe.
b check out the local nightlife together sometime.
c get a bike so that you can cycle to work?
d planting some flowers in your garden?
e use public transport more often.

8 ▶ **10.8** Complete the conversation. Circle the correct words. Listen and check your answers.

A: I really like living in Ottawa, but I don't like where we live now.

B: I know what you mean. Well, how about ¹*find / finding* a new neighbourhood?

A: Yeah. We could ²*move / moving* to the centre. The shopping is great there.

B: Yeah, but housing isn't very affordable. Maybe we could ³*move / moving* near the Greenbelt.

A: That's not a bad idea. Tom lives there.

B: Why don't you ⁴*ask / asking* him what it's like?

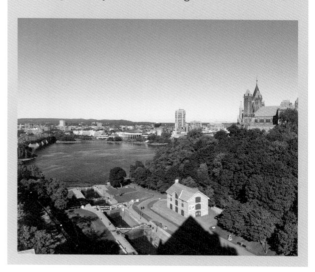

9 Complete each suggestion with ideas about your own city.

1 A: I want to live in a fun, exciting part of the city.
  B: You should _____.

2 A: I'd love to move to an area with a lot of green space.
  B: Maybe you could _____.

3 A: I want to find a cheap flat in the centre as quickly as possible.
  B: Why don't you _____?

SPEAKING The right part of town

10 Work in pairs. Student A: Turn to page 151. Student B: Turn to page 155. Do the roleplay.

10.3 Reshaping a city

READING Breathing new life into the old place

1 Read the first paragraph of the article. What problems on the South Side of Chicago are mentioned? Discuss with a partner.

BREATHING NEW LIFE INTO THE OLD PLACE

1 The South Side of Chicago is a part of the city that [1]has seen better days. Crime is a problem and there are few jobs. Many **blocks** contain empty buildings. But one **resident** is using his art
5 to bring new life to the place.

2 Theaster Gates saw the **decline** of his neighbourhood first-hand. As he grew up, he watched as buildings were [2]demolished by the local government or abandoned by their
10 owners. But as a [3]potter, Gates knew how to make beautiful things from very little. In 2008, he decided to buy an empty house not far from his own home, and he started to **renovate** it.

3 He used the house to **stage** [4]exhibitions
15 and meetings, and the site soon attracted many visitors. The success of the project led Gates to buy more properties – turning them into cultural centres and meeting places. As Gates says,

'We were slowly starting to reshape how people imagined the South Side of the city.' 20

4 One building, named Listening House, has a collection of old books that were donated by [5]publishing companies and bookshops. Another building was turned into a cinema and named Black Cinema House. It became so popular that 25 soon there wasn't enough room for all the visitors and a new **location** needed to be found.

5 Gates is now a well-known international artist. He has taken part in art shows in Germany and the United Kingdom, and in 2014 he was 30 named as one of the most powerful people in [6]contemporary art by *Art Review* magazine. But Gates never forgets his own neighbourhood, and his work in Chicago continues. He has even helped design a million-dollar art project for one of 35 the South Side's subway stations.

---

[1] **have seen better days (phrase)** be in a bad condition

[2] **demolish (v)** to completely destroy something

[3] **potter (n)** a person who makes pots, dishes, etc., from clay

[4] **exhibition (n)** an event in which art is shown to the public

[5] **publishing companies (n)** businesses that make books

[6] **contemporary art (n)** art made by artists working now

Understanding purpose

2 ▶ 10.9 Read the article. Match each paragraph with its purpose.

Paragraph 1   **a** explains why Theaster Gates started his first renovation project.

Paragraph 2   **b** describes how Gates's first project led to more.

Paragraph 3   **c** introduces and describes Chicago's South Side.

Paragraph 4   **d** gives examples of two of Gates's projects in Chicago.

Paragraph 5   **e** describes how Gates continues to work in Chicago despite international fame.

Understanding details

3 Are the following statements true, false or not given according to the article? Circle **T** for true, **F** for false or **NG** for not given.

1 Theaster Gates grew up in Chicago.   T   F   NG

2 The first house Gates renovated was near his home.   T   F   NG

3 Listening House is much bigger than Black Cinema House.   T   F   NG

4 Few people visited Black Cinema House.   T   F   NG

5 Gates has had art shows in Europe.   T   F   NG

6 He continues to work in Chicago.   T   F   NG

Understanding vocabulary

4 Match the words in **bold** from the article to their definitions.

1 **block**   **a** to organize (an event)

2 **resident**   **b** to make repairs to improve a building's condition

3 **decline**   **c** someone who lives in a particular place

4 **renovate**   **d** an area of land with streets on all its sides

5 **stage**   **e** a place where something happens

6 **location**   **f** a decrease in quality or importance

5 In what other ways could you renovate an empty building to create a cultural centre? Discuss with a partner.

Theaster Gates's first renovated property in his neighbourhood

10.4 How to revive a neighbourhood ...

TEDTALKS

1 Read the paragraph. Complete the definition of each **bold** word (1–4). You will hear these words in the TED Talk.

> **THEASTER GATES** decided to **tackle** his Chicago neighbourhood's problems by **reshaping** and reimagining **abandoned** buildings. His idea worth spreading is that art can be **a force for** social change, bringing new life to buildings, neighbourhoods and entire cities.

1 When you **tackle** a problem, you *ignore / deal with* it.

2 To **reshape** something means to *make a copy / change the structure* of it.

3 An **abandoned** building is one that the owner has *left empty / just bought*.

4 Something that is **a force for** change is *likely / unlikely* to make change happen.

2 ▶ 10.10 Watch Part 1 of the TED Talk. What problem in his neighbourhood does Theaster Gates talk about?

a high crime   **b** empty buildings   **c** not many jobs

3 ▶ 10.11 Watch Part 2 of the TED Talk. Complete the timeline with the events (a–f). One event is extra.

a Gates renovated the building.

b Gates bought other buildings.

c Gates got a new job to earn money.

d Gates began to sweep as a kind of performance art.

e People started to come to Gates's building.

f Gates used the building to stage exhibitions.

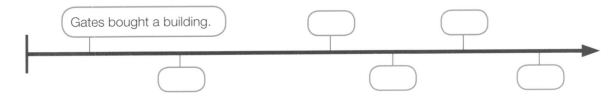

Gates bought a building.

4 ▶ 10.12 Watch Part 3 of the TED Talk. Circle the correct options to complete the sentences.

1 The Arts Bank project was difficult to finance because *no one was interested in the neighbourhood / the costs were very high*.

2 The Arts Bank is now used as a *free school for adults / place for exhibitions and performances*.

3 Theaster Gates is now *giving advice to others / doing art exhibitions* around the country.

CRITICAL THINKING

5 Work in pairs. Look at the diagram from the talk. Match a–e with the places (1–5). What does the diagram show?

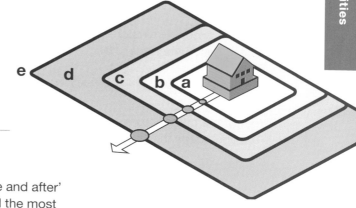

1 city _____

2 block _____

3 country _____

4 world _____

5 neighbourhood _____

6 Gates uses other images of old buildings and a 'before and after' photo of one of his buildings. Which image do you find the most powerful? Why?

VOCABULARY IN CONTEXT

7 ▶ 10.13 Watch the clips from the TED Talk. Choose the correct meaning of the words.

8 Work in pairs. Discuss the questions.

1 Can you think of something you enjoy that you no longer do?

2 Is there a building in your town that you would like to turn into something else?

PRESENTATION SKILLS Paraphrasing key points

> **TIPS**
>
> When giving a presentation, speakers often paraphrase their key points to make sure the audience understands. When you paraphrase, you repeat the same point but use different words.

9 ▶ 10.14 Watch the clip. Complete the sentence with the words you hear. Notice how Theaster Gates paraphrases his key point.

'In some ways, it feels very much like I'm a potter, that we tackle the things that are at our wheel, we _____ with the _____ that we have to think about this next bowl that I want to make.'

10 ▶ 10.15 Match the two parts to make sentences from the talk. Watch the clip to check your answers.

1 'It was dirt. It was nothing.

2 'We tricked it out.

3 '... we brought some heat,

4 '... how to start with what you got,

a how to start with the things that are in front of you.'

b It was nowhere.'

c We made it as beautiful as we could.'

d ... we kind of made a fire.'

11 Paraphrase these sentences. Compare your ideas with a partner.

1 The most important thing about the area you live in is safety.

2 The area I live in is really green.

10.5 Let's make things better

COMMUNICATE Planning improvements

1 A city has some problems in one of its neighbourhoods, and many of the residents are unhappy. You have been asked by the local government to plan some changes to solve the problems. Turn to page 154, look at the map and read about the problems.

2 Work in a group. Brainstorm ideas for improvements together. Choose the best suggestions to make a plan. Sketch the changes you want to make on the map.

> OK. I think we should build a park somewhere.   Good idea. How about here, near the river?

3 Work with a person from another group. Explain the changes that your group wants to make. Were your ideas the same or different?

DESCRIBING STEPS

First, … / Firstly, …
Second, … / Secondly, …
Third, … / Thirdly, …

WRITING Writing a proposal

4 Imagine your town or city wants to renovate a large old building in the centre. They are asking the community to suggest creative ideas for how to use the building. Write some suggestions.

> I have a good idea for how to use the building. We could turn it into a museum and tell the history of our town. We could also organize interesting activities, like music and art classes …

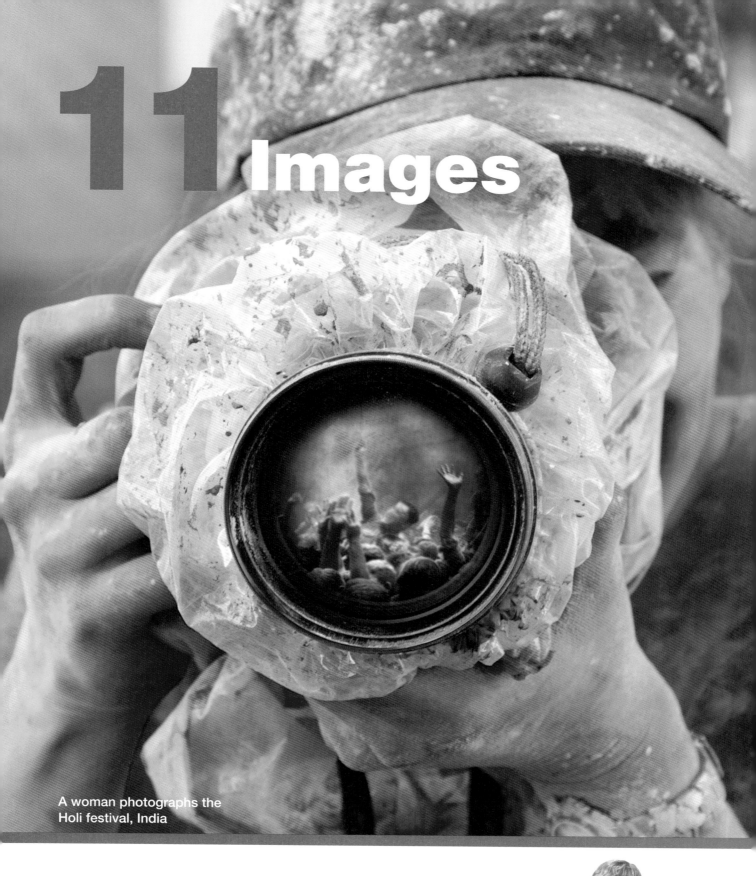

11 Images

A woman photographs the
Holi festival, India

WARM UP

Look at the photo and read the caption. Discuss
the questions.

1 What do you think of this photograph? Why?

2 What do we learn about the Holi festival from this
image?

3 Do you enjoy taking photographs? What kind?

In this unit you:

* talk about photographs
* give opinions
* watch a TED
  Talk by **ERIK
  JOHANSSON**

115

Photographer Erik Johansson creates striking images that seem impossible

11.1 Snapshots

VOCABULARY Photography

1 Add these words to the word map.

| background | beautiful | camera | landscape | picture | shape | weird |

Types
portrait, wildlife,
_____

Other words for *photo*
shot, image,
_____

Equipment
lens, flash,
_____

PHOTOGRAPHY

Aspects
colour, space,
perspective, light,
_____

Opinions of photos
strange, stunning, boring,
_____

2 Work in pairs. Look at the photo on this page. Describe the photo and say what you like about it.

It's a bit strange, but I really like it.

Me too. I love the background.

LISTENING My perfect photo

> **Listening for opinions**
> When you listen for a speaker's opinion, listen for verbs like *think, believe, feel, seems* and for expressions like *to me* and *in my opinion*.

3 ▶ **11.1** Listen to photographer Hannah Reyes talking about what is important when taking a photo. Tick (✓) the things she talks about.

   a using the right equipment

   b being in the right place

   c understanding light

4 ▶ **11.1** Listen again. What's Hannah's favourite photo? Why does she like it?

5 What things do you consider when taking a photo? Discuss with a partner.

Hannah Reyes

Pronunciation Compound words

6a ▶ **11.2** Listen to how the two parts of the words in **bold** sound in this extract.

… and it reminds me of the wonders of **childhood**, when everything felt like a giant **playground**.

6b ▶ **11.3** Listen and repeat these words.

   1 landscape   **2** background   **3** wildlife   **4** snapshot

SPEAKING What do you think?

7 ▶ **11.4** Listen to the conversation. A man and a woman are talking about the photo on page 116. Which person likes it more?

A: Hey, look at this **picture**.   **image / photo**

B: Wow! That's pretty cool.

A: It's really **unusual**, isn't it?   **strange / weird**

B: Yeah.

A: I love the colours and the **use of space**.   **background / perspective**

B: Yeah. But I think anyone can make a picture like this with a computer.

A: I don't think so. **I think** you still need real talent.   **In my opinion, / To me,**

B: I know what you mean. But I find real photos more interesting.

8 Practise the conversation with a partner. Practise again using the words on the right.

9 Work in a group. Find a photo you like on your phone. Describe the photo and say what you like about it. Use the words in Exercise 1.

I like this photo. I took it a few weeks ago in the park. I like the colours and the light.

Yes, it's beautiful.

11.2 What's your opinion?

HOW TO TELL IF A PHOTO IS NOT REAL

Modern technology makes it possible to create and change images very easily. How can you tell if a photo is not real? Ask yourself these four questions.

Are there any differences in the lighting and shadows?

Is anything in the photo too big or too small?

Are there any strangely curved or bending surfaces?

Use your common sense – is anything else unusual?

GRAMMAR *look* and *look like*

1 ▶ 11.5 Look at the infographic. Then look at the photo on page 119. Do you think the image is real or digitally altered? Discuss with a partner.

2 ▶ 11.6 Listen to two people discussing the image on page 119. Why do they think the image is not real?

3 Read the sentences in the Grammar box. Choose the correct options to complete a and b.

LOOK AND LOOK LIKE

Wow. It **looks** real.

It **looks like** a fake, to me.

a *Look* is always followed by *a noun / an adjective*.

b *Look like* is always followed by *a noun / an adjective*.

Check your answers on page 147 and do Exercise 1.

4 Complete the sentences with the correct form of *look* or *look like*.

1 It's very tall and made of metal and people come from all over the world to visit it. To me, it _____ stunning but when it was first built, many people thought it _____ ugly.

2 It's a statue. It _____ a woman wearing a large crown and holding a torch. Tourists can climb up to visit her head. She _____ strong and powerful.

3 You can stay here – in the tallest building in the world. The designers wanted it to _____ the spider lily flower. It makes all the buildings around it _____ very small!

5 What place or building do you think is being described in each sentence in Exercise 4?

LANGUAGE FOCUS Asking for and giving opinions

6 ▶ **11.7** Study the examples in the Language focus box.

ASKING FOR AND GIVING OPINIONS

Do you think this photo is interesting?

Yes, I **do**. I **think** it's very interesting.
No, I **don't**. I **don't think** it's interesting.

What do you think of this image?
How do you feel about this picture?
What's your opinion of this shot?

I
think (that) it's amazing.
find it boring.

It
looks like a painting.
looks fake.
seems unreal.

To me, it's kind of weird.
In my opinion, it's stunning.

For more information and practice, go to page 147.

---

7 Complete the questions and answers.

1 A: (how / feel / this picture)
How do you feel about this picture? ?

B: (think / gorgeous)
_____ .

2 A: (what / think / this landscape)
_____ ?

B: (find / a little boring)
_____ .

3 A: (what / opinion / this portrait)
_____ ?

B: (not / think / real)
_____ .

4 A: (do / this picture / weird)
_____ ?

B: (yes / seems / strange)
_____ .

8 ▶ **11.8** Complete the information. Circle the correct words. Listen and check your answers.

Look at this photo. It ¹*looks / looks like* a giant sink. What ²*are you / do you* think? Is it real or digitally altered?

At first glance, the image ³*looks / looks like* quite realistic. But take a closer look at the shadows and lighting, and you'll probably ⁴*feel / look* that something is not quite right.

With today's technology, it's not difficult to create a photo like this one and make people believe ⁵*that / like* it's real. This image was made by combining two simple photos – one of a young boy and one of a bathroom sink. The sink ⁶*looks / looks like* huge when compared to the size of the boy.

Pronunciation Stress with opinions

9 ▶ **11.9** Listen. Notice where the stress is.

A: Do you think this photo is interesting?

B: Yes I do. I think it's very interesting.

C: I find it boring.

D: To me, it's kind of weird.

E: In my opinion, it's stunning.

SPEAKING Is it real?

10 Choose two photos in the book. Work in pairs. Ask for and give opinions on the photos.

11 Turn to page 155 and look at the two photos. One is digitally altered and one is real. Use the questions in the infographic to decide which one is real. Discuss your ideas.

I think this one is real and this one is fake.

Why do you think so? It looks real to me.

119

11.3 Art and nature

READING When reality is stranger than fiction

1 Look at the title of the article and the two photos. What do you think the article is mainly about?

    a two photo contest winners   **b** famous fake photos   **c** amazing photos of nature

2 Read the first paragraph of the article. Check your prediction.

Photo of camel thorn trees by Frans Lanting

WHEN REALITY IS STRANGER THAN **FICTION**

These days, even an **amateur** photographer – using only a smartphone – can take a simple picture and transform it into a thing of beauty. The photos here, however, are a reminder that
5 perhaps the most amazing images are not those **enhanced** by computer software, but created by nature itself.

PHOTO OF CAMEL THORN TREES BY FRANS LANTING

10 Frans Lanting **captured** this stunning landscape image of camel thorn trees in a location called Dead Vlei in Namibia. Because of the lighting in the frame, the photograph looks like a painting.

In the photo, the trees appear against a bright
15 background. The background appears to be an orange-coloured sky, but it is in fact a [1]sand dune dotted with white grasses. Lanting got the shot at **dawn** when the light of the morning sun lit up the dune. The ground looks blue because it is reflecting the colour of the sky above.   20

PHOTO OF CAMEL SHADOWS BY CHRIS JOHNS

Chris Johns shot this photo of a group of camels crossing the desert near Lake Assal in Djibouti, one of the lowest points on Earth.   25

The camels appear dark against the light-coloured sand. However, what the viewer sees as a camel is actually its **shadow**. The camels are the thin brown lines. Johns took the photo from straight above the animals. The late afternoon sun casts   30 the long shadows.

---

[1] **sand dune (n)** a large hill of sand formed by the wind

Understanding main ideas

3 ▶ 11.10 Read the article. Tick (✓) the statements that you think the author would agree with.

a Modern technology makes it easy for people to create a beautiful photo.

b Computer-produced images are now more amazing than real photographs.

c The photos mentioned in the article show that you don't need a computer to create amazing images.

Understanding details

4 Complete the Venn diagram using the information (a–f).

a taken in Africa

b taken in the morning

c taken in the afternoon

d taken from above

e uses sand as a background

f taken from the ground

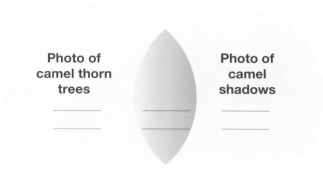

Photo of camel thorn trees   Photo of camel shadows

5 Circle the correct options to complete the sentences.

1 When Frans Lanting took the photo, the sky was *orange / blue*.

2 The thin brown lines in Chris Johns' photo are *camels / shadows*.

Understanding vocabulary

6 Complete the definitions.

1 If you **enhance** something, you make it *better / worse*.

2 If you are an **amateur**, you *get paid / don't get paid* for what you do.

3 You can **capture** an image with a *camera / book*.

4 **Dawn** is in the *morning / evening*.

5 You make a **shadow** by blocking *sound / light*.

7 Which photo from the article do you think was more difficult to capture? Why? Discuss with a partner.

Photo of camel shadows by Chris Johns

11.4 Impossible photography

TEDTALKS

1 Read the paragraph. Match each **bold** word to its meaning (1–4). You will hear these words in the TED Talk.

> **ERIK JOHANSSON** loves to **combine** photos to create a **realistic**-looking image –
> but one that is often a kind of **illusion**. His idea worth spreading is that photography
> can be a highly creative medium that **tricks** the eye and captures an idea, rather than
> an actual moment or place.

1 not fake-looking: _____

2 something that seems real but isn't: _____

3 deceives or fools: _____

4 join together: _____

2 ▶ **11.11** Watch Part 1 of the TED Talk. Circle the correct options to complete the sentences.

1 Erik Johansson's passion for photography mixed with his earlier interest in *drawing / computers*.

2 He says that with normal photographs the process *starts / ends* when you take the photo.

3 In Johansson's images, most of the work is done *before / after* he takes the photo.

3 ▶ **11.12** Watch Part 2 of the TED Talk. Complete the notes.

To create a realistic combined photo:

1 The two photos should have the same _____ .

2 The two photos should have the same type of _____ .

3 It should be impossible to see where one photo _____ and the other
_____ . In other words, the two photos should be seamless.

4 ▶ **11.13** Watch Part 3 of the TED Talk. Tick (✓) the statement(s) that Erik Johansson would agree with.

a It's important to plan very carefully.

b Any two photos can be combined with a realistic result.

c Today's technology is not yet good enough to create realistic looking images.

CRITICAL THINKING

5 In the talk, Erik Johansson says, 'It felt like photography was more about being at the right place at the right time. I felt like anyone could do that.' Do you agree? Discuss with a partner.

VOCABULARY IN CONTEXT

6 ▶ 11.14 Watch the clips from the TED Talk. Choose the correct meaning of the words.

7 Work in pairs. Discuss the questions.

1 Can you think of a time when you were in the right place at the right time?

2 Think of an activity you enjoy. What rules do you need to remember when you do it?

PRESENTATION SKILLS Introducing a visual

Speakers often show visuals – photos, maps, charts, videos – to support their talks. Here are some ways to introduce a visual.

Here's a picture/video of …
In this …
I'd like to show you …

This is a chart/map of …
I want to share with you …
Take a look at …

8 ▶ 11.15 Watch the clip of Erik Johansson introducing a visual. Complete the sentences.

'I'm here to ¹_____ my photography. Or is it photography? Because, of course,

²_____ is a ³_____ that you can't take with your camera.'

9 ▶ 11.16 Now watch other TED speakers introduce visuals. Tick (✓) the expressions you hear.

a This is …

c Here's …

e In this …

b Have a look.

d I want to show you …

f Let's have a look at …

10 Work in a group. Show your group members a photo or video from your phone. Say what it is.

11.5 Look again!

COMMUNICATE Discussing combinations

1 Work in pairs. Look at the photos. Each photo shows a real animal which combines two other animals. Which two? Label the photos with these words.

camel	donkey	lion	sheep	whale
dolphin	goat	llama	tiger	zebra

_____ + _____

_____ + _____

_____ + _____

_____ + _____

_____ + _____

2 Choose two animals to combine. Give it a name and discuss what's interesting about it.

> We could combine a dog and a penguin. We can call it a denguin.

> Great idea! It can have the body of a dog and wings and feet like a penguin.

ASKING ABOUT SPELLING

How do you spell that?	D-E-N-G-U-I-N.
Is that spelled with a *d* or a *p*?	It's spelled with a *d*, as in *dog*.

WRITING Describing a photo

3 Search online, or in this book, for a photo that you really like. Write a description of it. Explain what the photo shows and what you like about it.

> I really like this photo on page 36. It shows a surfer in freezing cold water. I love the lighting and the perspective. Just looking at the photo makes me feel cold.

12 Health

Friends enjoy the healthy effect
of the mud in the Dead Sea

WARM UP

Look at the photo and read the caption. Discuss
the questions.

1 How do you think the mud makes the woman feel?

2 Do you think it is good for her health? Why? /
Why not?

3 What other kinds of places are good for your health?

In this unit you:

- discuss healthy and
  unhealthy habits
- talk about facts
- watch a TED Talk
  by **MYRIAM
  SIDIBE**

Thousand of people doing yoga
at Red Rocks Park, Colorado

12.1 Staying healthy

VOCABULARY Habits

1 Match the words in each set.

1 wash	**a** sugar-free soft drinks	**7** avoid	**a** vitamins
2 go	**b** your hands	**8** get	**b** red meat
3 drink	**c** to the gym	**9** take	**c** eight hours of sleep

4 eat	**a** fruit every day	**10** do	**a** a bike
5 brush	**b** mouthwash	**11** ride	**b** breakfast
6 use	**c** your teeth	**12** skip	**c** yoga

2 In your opinion, are the things in Exercise 1 good for your health, bad for your health, or do they make no difference? Complete the table. Then compare your opinions with a partner.

Healthy	Makes no difference	Unhealthy

3 Work in pairs. Share what you do to stay healthy.

I go to the gym and drink sugar-free soft drinks.

I go to the gym too. But I think sugar-free drinks are unhealthy. I try to drink water instead.

LISTENING My healthy (and unhealthy) habits

> **Recognizing linking sounds**
> When we speak, we don't usually say – each – word – separately.
> Instead, we join, or link, words together. If you can recognize linking,
> it will increase your comprehension.
>
>   take a vitamin   eight hours of sleep   have unhealthy habits

4 ▶ **12.1** Listen to David Matijasevich talking about some
of his habits. What does he say he does too much?

5 ▶ **12.1** Listen again. Complete the notes about David's habits.

Unhealthy habits	Healthy habits
• He drinks too much _____. • He doesn't _____ enough.	• He never _____. • He takes _____. • He exercises. For example, he _____ and plays _____.

Pronunciation Word linking (2)

6 ▶ **12.2** Listen to these phrases. Mark which words link together in informal speech.
Listen again and repeat.

1 drink at least

2 become a habit

3 has an effect

4 never eat snacks

SPEAKING Is that healthy?

7 ▶ **12.3** Listen to the conversation. Why doesn't speaker B drink sugar-free soft drinks?

A: Do you want a soft drink?

B: Just water, thanks. I don't drink soft drinks anymore.

A: Really? **Why not?**   **How come? / What's the reason?**

B: **When** you drink one fizzy drink, you consume   **If / Every time**
eight teaspoons of sugar.

A: Wow! Well, I have some sugar-free soft drinks.

B: Oh, **someone told me** that's even worse. I don't   **apparently / I heard**
think sugar substitutes are **good for your health**.   **very healthy / good for you**

A: OK, but I only have tap water. Is that OK?

B: You know, I'm not that thirsty actually.

8 Practise the conversation with a partner. Practise again using the words on the right.

9 Work in pairs. What kind of food or drink do you avoid? Explain your reasons.

> I try to avoid eating fast food. It's really unhealthy.

> Yeah, me too. I also avoid drinking too much coffee.

12.2 Healthy choices

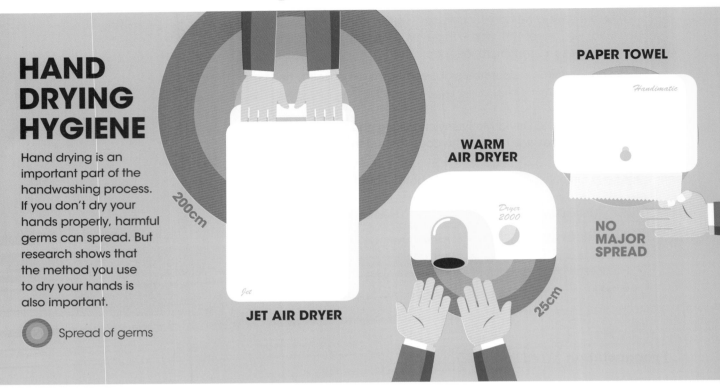

HAND DRYING HYGIENE

Hand drying is an important part of the handwashing process. If you don't dry your hands properly, harmful germs can spread. But research shows that the method you use to dry your hands is also important.

○ Spread of germs

200cm

JET AIR DRYER

WARM AIR DRYER

Dryer 2000

25cm

PAPER TOWEL

Handimatic

NO MAJOR SPREAD

GRAMMAR Zero conditional

1 ▶ **12.4** Look at the infographic. What's the best method for drying your hands? Why?

2 ▶ **12.5** Listen to an expert discuss hand drying. Complete the sentences.

1 The expert says that when she dries her hands, she always uses a _____ .

2 A _____ may not make your hands completely dry.

3 A _____ can spread germs around.

3 Read the sentences in the Grammar box. Answer the questions (a and b).

4 Complete the paragraph using these words.

know	need	shake
wash	use	want

UK government guidelines say if you
¹_____ to get your hands really clean, you should ²_____ your hands for not five, not ten, but twenty seconds! If you ³_____ soap and water and remember to wash the backs of your hands and between your fingers, then you ⁴_____ your hands are really clean! Also, if you ⁵_____ your hands twelve times before you dry them on a paper towel, you only ⁶_____ to use one towel. This is much better for the environment.

ZERO CONDITIONAL

If you **don't** dry your hands at all, germs **can** spread very easily.

When you **use** a paper towel, germs **don't get** blown around.

a Do we use zero conditional sentences to say something is always true or sometimes true?

b What tense do we use in each part of the sentence?

Check your answers on page 148 and do Exercise 1.

LANGUAGE FOCUS Talking about facts

5 ▶ **12.6** Study the examples in the Language focus box.

TALKING ABOUT FACTS

If/When you **drink** one fizzy drink, you **consume** eight teaspoons of sugar.

You **consume** eight teaspoons of sugar **if/when** you **drink** one fizzy drink.

What happens **if/when** you dry your hands with a warm air dryer?

If/When you dry your hands with a warm air dryer, what happens?

When
Whenever   I **dry** my hands, I **use** a paper towel.
Every time

For more information and practice, go to page 148.

6 Put the words and phrases in the correct order to make sentences.

1 it relaxes / have a hot bath / When / your whole body / you

2 a healthy breakfast / eat / If / energy for the day / it gives you / you

3 get stronger / lift weights regularly / if / Your muscles / you

7 ▶ **12.7** Complete the information. Use the correct form of the verbs. Listen and check your answers.

Hand sanitizers are everywhere these days, but are they a good thing?

In short, yes, but be careful. Any hand sanitizer should contain at least 60 per cent alcohol. If it ¹_____ (contain) less, it ²_____ (not kill) harmful bacteria.

Hand sanitizers are certainly convenient, but they should not replace regular handwashing. For example, if your hands ³_____ (be) very dirty, it ⁴_____ (be) much better to wash them with soap and water.

Also, be careful not to use hand sanitizers too often. When you ⁵_____ (overuse) sanitizer, the alcohol ⁶_____ (dry) out your skin.

Pronunciation Listening for unstressed words

8 ▶ **12.8** Listen. Try to complete the sentences.

1 If _____ tired, I _____ a walk makes me _____ better.

2 When I _____ to bed before eleven, I find _____ easier to get _____ sleep.

3 If _____ drink lots _____ water, it helps _____ brain to stay focused.

SPEAKING Healthy choices

9 Read the sentences. Do you think these are healthy choices? Discuss with a partner.

'If I need a snack, I eat something low in sugar.'

'When I feel stressed, I play computer games.'

'If I feel ill, I go to bed early and rest.'

'When I feel tired in the evening, I drink coffee.'

10 Find out what your partner does in the situations in Exercise 9.

What do you do if you need a snack?

I try not to eat anything. If I'm really hungry, I eat something healthy.

12.3 A simple solution

READING Learning to use 'the most beautiful invention'

1 Read the first paragraph of the article. What is the article mainly about?

    a the work of a public health expert in Africa   **b** why people take part in Global Handwashing Day

LEARNING TO USE 'THE MOST BEAUTIFUL INVENTION'

1 Every year on 15th October, over 200 million people around the world take part in **Global** Handwashing Day. But why dedicate a day to something we do all the time? Well, research
5 shows that not enough people regularly wash their hands with soap. Experts believe that this leads to the deaths of millions of people every year.

2 Myriam Sidibe says that soap is 'the most beautiful invention in public health'. As a public
10 health expert, Sidibe knows that washing your hands with soap can have a huge impact on reducing [1]flu, [2]cholera and the **spread** of other diseases. It can reduce [3]diarrhoea by half and [4]respiratory infections by one third. Handwashing
15 with soap **prevents** babies from getting ill and keeps children healthy and in school.

3 However, washing hands with soap does not occur as **frequently** as you might think. This is partly due to a lack of resources in poorer

countries, but it's also because for many people, 20 handwashing is simply not part of their everyday routine. It's not easy to get people to change habits they learned in early childhood – but this is what Global Handwashing Day wants to do.

4 In 2008, the Indian cricket team joined around 25 100 million Indian schoolchildren in washing their hands to promote the first ever Global Handwashing Day. Every year since then, the campaign has held many different events around the world. In 2014, Global Handwashing Day was 30 used in the fight against Ebola, with events held in affected African countries.

5 Today, local and national leaders continue to use the day to spread the message about the importance of clean hands. The hope is that 35 handwashing becomes a regular part of people's lives and makes a **vital** difference to the health of millions around the world.

---

[1] **flu (n)** (short for **influenza**) a common illness that makes you feel hot (or cold), weak and tired

[2] **cholera (n)** a serious disease that affects your stomach and small intestine

[3] **diarrhoea (n)** an illness that causes you to pass waste from your body frequently

[4] **respiratory infection (n)** a disease that affects your breathing

Understanding purpose

2 ▶ 12.9 Read the article. Match each paragraph to its purpose (a–e).

1	Paragraph 1	**a**	suggests why many people don't wash their hands.
2	Paragraph 2	**b**	describes what Global Handwashing Day hopes to achieve.
3	Paragraph 3	**c**	describes the benefits of handwashing with soap.
4	Paragraph 4	**d**	gives examples of Global Handwashing Day events.
5	Paragraph 5	**e**	introduces Global Handwashing Day.

Understanding details

3 Answer the questions. Tick (✓) all answers that apply.

1 Which aims of Global Handwashing Day are mentioned in the article?

a to teach people about the importance of handwashing

b to make people use less water when they wash their hands

c to make handwashing part of everyone's routine

2 Which benefits of handwashing with soap are mentioned?

a Children miss fewer days of school because they're healthier.

b It prevents us from catching diseases from animals.

c It stops us spreading diseases to babies.

3 According to the article, what is challenging about getting people to wash their hands?

a It's hard to change habits.

b People often ignore advice about health.

c People don't trust their governments.

Understanding vocabulary

4 Match the **bold** words from the article to their definitions.

1	**global**	**a**	to keep something from happening
2	**prevent**	**b**	involving the whole world
3	**vital**	**c**	absolutely necessary

5 Choose the correct options to complete the sentences.

1 The **spread** of a disease refers to the disease _____ .

a decreasing   b increasing

2 If something happens **frequently**, it happens _____ .

a often   b rarely

Global Handwashing Day aims to make handwashing part of everyone's routine

6 What other things can people do to help prevent the spread of diseases? Discuss with a partner.

12.4 The simple power of handwashing

TEDTALKS

1 Read the paragraph. Choose the correct meaning of each bold word (1–3). You will hear these words in the TED Talk.

> **MYRIAM SIDIBE** grew up in Mali and is a public health expert. She feels we don't always need new technological **innovations** to prevent the spread of diseases. Her idea worth spreading is that if soap is **available** and that if people change their handwashing habits, we can greatly reduce disease and child **mortality** around the world.

    1 An **innovation** is a *new / traditional* idea or method.

    2 If something is **available**, it means it's easy to *find / use*.

    3 **Mortality** refers to the *birth / death* of people or animals.

2 ▶ **12.10** Watch Part 1 of the TED Talk. Answer the questions.

    1 What is a main cause of death for children under five years old?

      a plane crashes

      b disease

    2 According to Myriam Sidibe, handwashing with soap can save how many children every year?

3 ▶ **12.11** Watch Part 2 of the TED Talk. Complete the summary with these words. Four words are extra.

diseases	five	high	TVs	waste
dishes	free	ten	wash	week

Around the world, four out of ¹_____ people don't wash their hands after they use the toilet. This is true for countries where child mortality is ²_____ . But it's also true in richer countries that have soap, running water and fancy toilets. In some poorer countries, it's because soap is used for laundry and washing ³_____ . Soap is available, but it's precious, so a family may keep it in a cupboard so that people don't ⁴_____ it. Some families wash their hands only once a day or even once a ⁵_____ . However, this causes children at home to pick up ⁶_____ more easily.

4 ▶ **12.12** Watch Part 3 of the TED Talk. Answer the questions.

  1 How many people has Sidibe's handwashing program reached?

  a over 8 million   b around 100 million   c over 180 million

  2 How many people does Sidibe's team hope to reach by 2020?

  a around 500 million   b around one billion   c around 5 billion

  3 The most important time to protect a child is during the first ...

  a month   b year   c five years

CRITICAL THINKING

5 Why do you think Myriam Sidibe told the story of the mother from Myanmar? Discuss with a partner.

VOCABULARY IN CONTEXT

6 ▶ **12.13** Watch the clips from the TED Talk. Choose the correct meaning of the words.

7 Work in pairs. Discuss the questions.

  1 Think of a good friend. Can you remember how you got to know them?

  2 Can you think of three things people are supposed to do to stay healthy? Do you do them?

PRESENTATION SKILLS Getting the audience's attention

TIPS

It's important to get the audience's attention at the start of a presentation. For example, you can:

• tell a personal story.   • give a surprising fact or statistic.

• ask an interesting question.   • show a photo or video.

• use an interesting quote.

8 ▶ **12.14** Watch the clip. How does Myriam Sidibe get the audience's attention?

  a She tells a story.   **b** She uses a quote.   **c** She gives a statistic.

9 ▶ **12.15** Can you remember how these TED speakers get their audience's attention? Match the speaker to the technique he or she uses. Then watch and check.

  1 Meaghan Ramsey   **a** uses a video.

  2 Chris Burkhard   **b** gives a statistic.

  3 Yves Rossy   **c** shows a photo and asks a question.

10 Work in a group. Imagine you are going to give a presentation on the correct way to brush your teeth. How would you get your audience's attention?

133

12.5 Fact or myth

COMMUNICATE A food hygiene quiz

1 Work in pairs. Read the sentences about food hygiene. Decide if each one is a fact or a myth. Explain your answers.

  1 You should always throw food away after the 'best before' date.
  Fact   Myth

  2 If you drop food on the floor, it's safe to eat if you pick it up quickly.
  Fact   Myth

  3 A wooden cutting board is more hygienic than a plastic one.
  Fact   Myth

  4 You need to wash raw chicken before you cook it.
  Fact   Myth

  5 A beef steak is safe to eat if only the outside is cooked.
  Fact   Myth

  6 A hamburger is safe to eat if only the outside is cooked.
  Fact   Myth

  7 In your fridge, it's important to keep uncooked food below cooked food.
  Fact   Myth

2 Turn to page 155 and read the answers. Was anything surprising? Discuss with your partner.

DISAGREEING POLITELY

I don't really agree.

Actually, I have a different idea.

Sorry, but I have to disagree.

I'm not quite sure about that.

WRITING Giving health tips

3 Imagine it's the time of year when a lot of people have flu. Read the health tips. Add three more tips to stop the spread of flu.

The most important thing to do is not share food or drinks. If you share food or drinks, you spread your germs. Another tip is to always cover your mouth when you cough or sneeze ...

MODEL PRESENTATION

1 Complete the transcript of the presentation using these words.

background	heavy	maybe	picture	second	space
believe	if	opinion	safe	should	take

Let me tell you about my neighbourhood – it's a place called Wallingden. Here you can see that it's quite a beautiful place. There is a lot of green ¹_____ , and it's a really nice place to live. But it has a problem.

²_____ a look at this photograph. This is a ³_____ of Market Street in the morning. You can see that the traffic is really ⁴_____ . Now, in the ⁵_____ of the image you can see a school bus. This road is right outside our local school. ⁶_____ children walk to school in the morning, they have no ⁷_____ place to cross this road. In my ⁸_____ , this is really dangerous.

I ⁹_____ there are two things the local government needs to do. First, they ¹⁰_____ build a pedestrian crossing near the school, so children can cross safely. ¹¹_____ , they need to do something to reduce the traffic to stop so many cars using this road. ¹²_____ they can build another road nearby.

But there's also something we can do. We need to write a letter to the local government to tell them about the problem. I really hope that they listen.

Thank you so much.

2 ▶ **P.4** Watch the presentation and check your answers.

3 ▶ **P.4** Review the list of presentation skills from units 1–12 below. Which does the speaker use? Tick (✓) them as you watch again.

Presentation skills: units 1–12

The speaker:
- introduces himself/herself ☐
- gets the audience's attention ☐
- uses good body language ☐
- introduces his/her topic ☐
- uses gestures ☐
- involves the audience ☐
- uses statistics ☐
- shows enthusiasm ☐
- uses pauses ☐
- paraphrases key points ☐
- uses visuals ☐
- thanks the audience ☐

YOUR TURN!

4 Plan a short presentation about a problem in your neighbourhood, city or country. Use some our all of these questions to make some notes. If you have a suitable photo you can use that too.

- What place are you going to talk about?
- What exactly is the problem?
- In your opinion, who needs to solve the problem?
- What exactly should they do?

5 Look at the Useful phrases box. Think about which ones you will need in your presentation.

USEFUL PHRASES

Qualities of a neighbourhood:

clean streets, affordable housing, heavy traffic, reliable public transport, friendly neighbours, high crime, good nightlife, green space

Giving opinions:

I think / believe / feel that … / To me, … / In my opinion, …

Making suggestions:

We should … / Maybe we can … / One thing we could do is …

Describing steps:

Firstly, … / Secondly, … / Thirdly, …

6 Work in pairs. Take turns giving your presentation using your notes. Use some of the presentation skills from units 1–12. As you listen, tick (✓) each skill your partner uses.

Presentation skills: units 1–12

The speaker …

• introduces himself/herself	☐	• uses statistics	☐
• gets the audience's attention	☐	• shows enthusiasm	☐
• uses good body language	☐	• uses pauses	☐
• introduces his/her topic	☐	• paraphrases key points	☐
• uses gestures	☐	• uses visuals	☐
• involves the audience	☐	• thanks the audience	☐

7 Give your partner some feedback on his or her talk. Try to include two things you liked, and one thing he or she can improve.

> That was great. You used pauses, and you used great visuals. But you didn't look at the audience enough.

GRAMMAR Present simple

Form

Affirmative	Negative
I/You/We/They **like** hip-hop.	I/You/We/They **don't like** hip-hop. (don't = do not)
He/She/It **likes** jazz.	He/She/It **doesn't like** jazz. (doesn't = does not)

Question	Short answer
Do I/you/we/they **like** hip-hop?	Yes, you/I/we/they **do**. No, you/I/we/they **don't**.
Does he/she/it **like** jazz?	Yes, he/she/it **does**. No, he/she/it **doesn't**.

Notice that in short answers we use *do* and *don't*, not the main verb.

> A: *Do you like country music?*
> B: *Yes,* **I do**. (not *Yes, Hike*.)

Spelling rules for *he/she/it*

Most verbs add -*s*:

> *like → likes, show → shows*

Verbs ending in -*s*, -*sh*, -*ch*, -*x* add -*es*:

> *watch → watches, finish → finishes*

Verbs ending with consonant +-*y change to* -*ies*:

> *try → tries*

Some irregular verbs

> *do → does, have → has, go → goes, be → is*

Use

We use the simple present to talk about:

- our likes and dislikes.
  *I **love** hip-hop.*

- our habits and routine.
  *I **listen** to music every day.*

- things that are always true.
  *I **come** from Brazil.*

EXERCISES

1 Complete the sentences with the present simple form of the verbs.

1 My brother _____ (go) to a lot of concerts.

2 What kind of films _____ your sister _____ (watch)?

3 My mother _____ (teach) music in a school.

4 My friend _____ (study) classical guitar.

5 My parents _____ (not play) the same kind of music.

6 This _____ (be) my favourite song.

2 Complete the questions and answers with *do*, *does*, *don't* or *doesn't*.

1 A: _____ you like jazz?
   B: Yes, I _____ . It's my favourite.

2 A: _____ your friend like R&B?
   B: Yes, he _____ . He loves it.

3 A: _____ your friends like K-pop?
   B: No, they _____ like it at all.

4 A: _____ your mother like rock music?
   B: No, she _____ . She hates it.

3 Choose the correct options to complete the text.

My friends [1]*love / loves* music, but they [2]*don't / doesn't* like the same thing. They [3]*has / have* very different tastes. Jeff [4]*like / likes* pop, but he [5]*don't / doesn't* like jazz. Dee [6]*hate / hates* pop, but she [7]*love / loves* jazz! As for me, I [8]*love / loves* R&B. I [9]*listen / listens* to it every day.

LANGUAGE FOCUS Talking about likes and interests

We can use *Wh-* questions (*what, where, how, etc.*) to ask about:

- the types of things someone likes or doesn't like.
  A: **What kind** of art **do** you **like**?
  B: *I like modern art.*
  A: **What kind** of music **don't** you **like**?
  B: *I don't like hip-hop.*

- someone's favourites.
  A: **Who's** your favourite musician?
  B: *David Bowie.*
  A: **What's** your brother's favourite painting?
  B: *I don't know. He doesn't like art very much!*

To talk about likes, we can say:

> *I **like** Picasso **a lot**.* (strong)
> *I **really like** the British artist, Bridget Riley.* (strong)
> *I **love** Van Gogh.* (very strong)

To talk about dislikes we can say:

> *I **don't** like science fiction films **very much**.* (not very strong)
> *I **don't** like horror films **at all**.* (strong)
> *I **hate** romantic comedies!* (very strong)

EXERCISE

1 Put the words in the correct order to make sentences or questions.

1 all / like / doesn't / at / music / my sister / pop

2 don't / what / books / kinds / like / you / of / ?

3 much / I / like / very / don't / opera

4 favourite / who / artist / your / is / wife's / ?

GRAMMAR Adverbs and expressions of frequency

Form

Adverbs of frequency

100% *I **always** do my food shopping on Saturday.*

usually

often

sometimes

hardly ever / rarely

0% *never*

The adverb of frequency goes before the main verb (but after the verb *to be*).

*I **often get** cheap vegetables from my local shop.*
*The vegetables **are often** cheap at my local shop.*

Expressions of frequency

I do my food shopping	**once**	a week.
	twice	
	three times	
I go to my local market	**every**	week.
		weekend.
		month.

Notice that expressions of frequency go at the end of the sentence.

Use

We use adverbs of frequency to say how often something happens.

*I **always** pay for things with cash.*

We can also use time expressions to express frequency.

*I buy a coffee **every morning / once a day**.*

EXERCISE

1 Rewrite each sentence using the adverb or expression of frequency.

1 I go shopping alone. (sometimes)
_____ .

2 We look for sale items. (usually)
_____ .

3 I spend money on myself. (hardly ever)
_____ .

4 My friends go shopping. (twice a week).
_____ .

5 You are at the shops! (always)
_____ !

6 I pay for my bus pass. (every month)
_____ .

LANGUAGE FOCUS Talking about habits and routines

To ask about frequency we can form two different kinds of questions:

• For *yes/no* answers we can use *do + ever*.
A: **Do** you **ever** spend money on designer shoes?
B: *No, I hardly ever spend money on expensive clothes.*

A: **Does** he **ever** download films?
B: *Yes, he sometimes downloads films.*

• To find out more exact information, we can use *how often*.
A: **How often** do you spend money on books and magazines?
B: *I buy a new book nearly every weekend.*

A: **How often** do your parents go shopping?
B: *They go shopping every Monday.*

EXERCISE

1 Write the correct question for each answer.

1 A: _____ .
B: No, I rarely go to a restaurant for lunch. I usually have a sandwich.

2 A: _____ .
B: I take a taxi about three times a year. Not very often!

3 A: _____ .
B: My brother? Yes, he often buys video games. He must spend a lot of money on them.

4 A: _____ .
B: I probably go away at weekends about twice a month.

GRAMMAR *like* and *would like*

Form

Affirmative	Negative
I **like** my job.	I **don't like** my job.
I **like** work**ing** here.	I **don't like** work**ing** here.
I**'d like to** work from home. (I'd = I would)	I **wouldn't like to** work from home.

Questions	Short answers
Do you **like** your job / work**ing** here?	Yes, I **do**. / No, I **don't**.
Would you **like to** get a new job?	Yes, I **would**. No, I **wouldn't**.

Use

To ask if someone likes or enjoys something now, we can use *do you like + ing*.

Do you like being *a dancer?*

To ask what someone wants to do in the future, we can use *would you like to + infinitive*.

Would you like to dance *for a big ballet company?*

EXERCISE

1 Complete the text with these words.

being	doesn't	to have
meeting	would	wouldn't

Ken Arnold has a new job as the director of a museum in Copenhagen. He really likes
¹_____ in a new city and ²_____ interesting people. But it's hard work and he
³_____ like being so busy and tired! When I ask him, '⁴_____ you like to go back to your old job?' He says, 'No, I ⁵_____ – I love this job, but I would like ⁶_____ more hours in the day!'

LANGUAGE FOCUS Asking about and describing jobs

To ask someone to describe something we can ask questions with *what + is ... like*.
> A: **What's** *your new office* **like**?
> B: *It's nice but it's pretty noisy.*
> A: **What are** *the hours* **like**?
> B: *They're not bad. I usually work 9–5.*

The usual question to ask about someone's job is:
What do you do?

The usual answers are *I'm a ...* or *I work in ...* .
> *I'm a teacher.* (to talk about your role)
> *I work in marketing/sales/education.* (to talk about an *area* of work)

EXERCISE

1 Complete the question for each answer.

1 A: What _____ your new job like?
   B: It's great!

2 A: What _____ you like about working here?
   B: It's really interesting.

3 A: What _____ you like about your job?
   B: The pay is pretty terrible.

4 A: What kind of job _____ you like to have one day?
   B: I'd like to work in politics.

5 A: What does your husband _____?
   B: He's a journalist.

GRAMMAR *can* and *can't*

Form

Affirmative	Negative
I **can** sing.	I **can't** dance.

Yes/no question	Short answers
Can you speak Korean?	Yes, I **can**. / No, I **can't**.

Wh- question	
What languages **can** you speak?	I **can** speak Spanish and English.

Use

We use *can* to talk about abilities we have and *can't* to talk about abilities we don't have.

   I can sing.   *I can't dance.*

We use the infinitive without *to* after *can*.

   I can drive.   *She can drive.*   *They can drive.*

EXERCISES

1 Rewrite each sentence using *can*.

  1 Jake is a dancer.

    _____ .

  2 Yazmira is a writer.

    _____ .

  3 Mary and Tom are singers.

    _____ .

  4 Nina is a runner.

    _____ .

  5 Paolo is a cook.

    _____ .

2 Choose the correct options to complete the questions. Then answer the questions.

  1 Can your best friend *dance / dances* well?

    _____ .

  2 What languages *you can / can you* speak?

    _____ .

  3 What sports can't you *play / to play*?

    _____ .

LANGUAGE FOCUS Describing abilities and talents

We can use *know how to* with the same meaning as *can* to talk about abilities.

  A: **Do** you **know how to** play the violin?
  B: *No, I don't. But I* **know how to** *play the ukulele!*

To describe how well we do something, we can add an adverb at the end of the sentence or clause.

  I don't speak Japanese very **well**, *but I can understand it* **easily**.

Notice that we form regular adverbs by adding *-ly* to the adjective. Adjectives ending in *-y* change to *-ily*. There are also some irregular adverbs (e.g. *good → well, fast → fast*).

To ask about ability we can ask these questions:

  What talents do you **have**?
  What are you **good at**? (more informal)

To ask someone if they can do something well we can use *be + good at +* noun or *-ing*.

  A: **Are** you **good at** play**ing** football?
  B: *No, I'm not. But I***'m** *quite* **good at** *table football!*

EXERCISE

1 Correct the mistake in the questions. Then answer the questions. Use positive (✓) or negative (✗) answers.

  1 Can your mother speak fluently Italian?

    (✓) _____ .

  2 Can you run fastly?

    (✗) _____ .

  3 Are you good in solving problems?

    (✓) _____ .

  4 Does he know how ride a motorbike?

    (✗) _____ .

GRAMMAR *much, many, a lot of*

Form

A: **How many** *songs do you have on your phone?*
B: *I have* **a lot**. */ I don't have* **many**.
A: **How much** *music do you have on your phone?*
B: *I have* **a lot**. */ I don't have* **much**.

You have a **lot of** *gadgets/technology!*
I don't have **many** *gadgets.*
I don't have **much** *technology.*

Use

We use *how many* to ask about countable things.

How many *of your* **friends** *are online now?*

We use *how much* to ask about uncountable things.

How much time *do we have?*

We can use *a lot of* for countable and uncountable things. Notice we can also use *a lot of* in negative sentences and questions.

I have **a lot of videos/time**.
I don't have **a lot of videos**.
Do you have **a lot of free time**?

We use *many* in negative sentences and questions for countable things.

I don't have **many videos**.
Do you have **many videos**?

We use *much* in negative sentences and questions for uncountable things.

I don't have **much time**.
Do you have **much time**?

EXERCISES

1 Write the words in the correct column of the table.

phones	time	money
memory	sleep	hours
people	computers	power

How many?	How much?

2 Choose the correct options to complete the sentences.

1 How *many / much* texts can you send a month?
2 I don't have much *money / euros* to spend on technology.
3 This doesn't hold *many / much* photos.

4 I don't have *many / much* space on my computer.
5 How much *memory / memories* does your laptop have?
6 My computer doesn't have *many / much* battery life.

LANGUAGE FOCUS Describing things and how they work

We use *much, many* and *a lot of* for big quantities and *a few* and *a little* for small quantities. We use *a little* with uncountable nouns and *a few* with countable nouns.

I have **a little** *money. I want to buy* **a few** *new songs.*

To describe what we use something for we can add *to* + infinitive.

I only use my phone **to make** *phone calls!*

To find out how something works we can ask what something *does*.

A: *What* **does** *this camera* **do**?
B: *It can take photos underwater.*

Only a little and *not much* have a similar meaning. *Only a few* and *not many* also have a similar meaning. *Not much* and *not many* are a little more negative.

A: *How much signal can you get on your phone here?*
B: **Only a little. / Not much**.
A: *How many people do you know who use wearable technology?*
B: **Only a few. / Not many**.

EXERCISE

1 Complete the sentences with one word.

1 A: How _____ do you use social media?
   B: Not _____. Only to communicate with my children!

2 A: How _____ contacts do you have on your phone?
   B: I have lots but I only use a _____!

3 A: What can this gadget _____?
   B: Well it can do different things. I usually use it _____ check the weather.

4 A: I have a _____ photos of the concert. Do you want to see them?
   B: Sure. I have a _____ time before class. Let's have a look!

GRAMMAR Time clauses

Form

Before *I visit a new country, I try to learn a few phrases of the language.*

When *I don't know a word in English, I look it up in a dictionary.*

After *I learn a new word, I write it in my notebook.*

Notice that we can also use *before* and *after* as prepositions.

> **Before** *visiting a new country, I try to learn a few phrases of the language.*
> **After** *every lesson, I write a list of new vocabulary in my notebook.*

We can use time clauses at the beginning or end of a sentence. Remember to use a comma when the time clause is at the start of the sentence.

> **When** *I have an exam, I get nervous.*
> *I get nervous* **when** *I have an exam.*

Use

I listen to relaxing music **before** I have an exam.

I have an exam.

When I have an exam, I get very stressed.

After I have an exam, I go out shopping.

EXERCISE

1 Use the time clauses to make sentences.

1 I take an exam / I eat a big breakfast (before)

_____ .

2 I try to go for a run / I feel stressed (when)

_____ .

3 I check my notes / I give a presentation (before)

_____ .

4 I get some advice from a friend / I feel better (after)

_____ .

5 I feel sleepy / I eat a big meal (after)

_____ .

6 I do well in an exam / I feel very happy (when)

_____ .

LANGUAGE FOCUS Describing sequence

We use the adverbs *first, then, next* and *after that* to describe the order we do something, especially in written language. *Then, next* and *after that* all have a similar meaning. We usually use a comma after them.

> **First**, *I find a comfortable chair.* **Next**, *I find a good pen.* **After that**, *I'm ready to start.*

We often use these adverbs in instructions.

> **First**, *read the questions carefully.* **Then**, *make some notes on the first question.*

EXERCISE

1 Choose the correct options to complete the text.

[1]*When / After* I feel stressed because I have a lot to do, I usually make a list. [2]*When / After that*, I do some breathing exercises. That helps to make me feel calm. [3]*Next / Before*, I do the first job on my list. [4]*When / Then*, I reward myself with a cup of coffee. [5]*After that, / After* I finish my coffee, I am ready to start the second job on my list!

Grammar summary | UNIT 7

GRAMMAR Comparatives and superlatives

Form

Comparatives		
Adjective	**Spelling**	**Example**
one-syllable	add -er add -r for adjectives that end in -e	deep → deep**er** wide → wid**er**
ending in one vowel + one consonant	double the consonant and add -er	big → big**ger**
most two- and all three-syllable	add *more* before the adjective	famous → **more** famous beautiful → **more** beautiful
two-syllable, ending in -y	change -y to -ier	pretty → prett**ier**

We use *than* after a comparative adjective.
> *The landscape here is more beautiful **than** in the north.*

Superlatives		
Adjective	**Spelling**	**Example**
one-syllable	add *the* + -est add -st for adjectives that end in -e	deep → **the** deep**est** wide → **the** wid**est**
ending in one vowel + one consonant	double the consonant and add *the* + -est	big → **the** big**gest**
most two- and all three-syllable	add *the most* before the adjective	famous → **the most** famous beautiful → **the most** beautiful
two-syllable, ending in -y	add *the* and change -y to -iest	pretty → **the** prett**iest**

We use *the* before a superlative adjective.
> *For me, desert landscapes are **the** most beautiful.*

Use

We use comparative adjectives to compare two things or people.
> *The Dutch are **taller** than the Norwegians.*

We use superlative adjectives to compare something to more than two other things and show that it has more of a particular quality than any others in the group.
> *The Dutch are **the tallest** people in the world.*

EXERCISES

1 Complete the sentences with the comparative form of the adjectives.

1 Tokyo is _____ (big) than Moscow.
2 Is Rio _____ (nice) in spring or autumn?
3 The Sahara is _____ (hot) than the Gobi Desert.
4 Is Sydney or Melbourne _____ (exciting)?
5 The Alps are _____ (pretty) than the Andes.
6 Do you think people in Canada are _____ (happy) than people in the United States?

2 Correct the mistake in each sentence.

1 They say that Denmark is the happyest country in the world.
2 Niger has the younger population of any country.
3 Chile has largest swimming pool in the world. It's 900 metres long!
4 The wetest places in the world are in Northern India.
5 Surveys show Switzerland is the more expensive country to live in.
6 The world's most small ocean is the Arctic.

LANGUAGE FOCUS Making comparisons

There are a few irregular comparative and superlative forms (e.g. *good → better → best, bad → worse → worst, far → further → furthest*).
> *The climate is **worse** here than in the south.*
> *This is the **best** country in the world!*

We can use comparatives and superlatives in questions.
> *Is it **better** to drive or take the train?*
> *Which city is the **furthest** from the sea?*

When we make comparisons, we can use *less* to mean the opposite of *more*.
> *It's **less** rainy in the spring than in the autumn.*

EXERCISE

1 Complete the sentences with the comparative or superlative form of these adjectives.

far	good	bad

1 It's much _____ to go by this route. It's an extra five kilometres!
2 This is my favourite time of year. It's the _____ time to see wild flowers and the weather is beautiful.
3 What is the _____ you can walk in one day?
4 Personally, I think it's _____ to visit in summer than in winter. The mosquitoes are terrible in the summer!

GRAMMAR Modifying adverbs

Form

*She's **extremely** talkative.*
*She's **very** / **really** happy.*
*She's **pretty** quiet.*
*She's **quite** short.*
*She's **fairly** shy.*
*She's **not very** tall.*

Strong

Weak

Use

Extremely, very and *really* make an adjective stronger.
*He's friendly. → He's **very** friendly.*

Pretty usually makes adjectives a little stronger.
*He's **pretty** friendly.*

Quite usually makes adjectives a little weaker.
*He's **quite** friendly.*

Fairly usually makes adjectives weaker.
*He's **fairly** friendly.*

Not very makes adjectives weak.
*She's **not very** old.*

Not very can also be a polite way to express a negative idea.
*He's **not very** friendly.* (Can often mean *He's unfriendly.*)

EXERCISE

1 Choose the correct option to make each adjective stronger (↕) or weaker (↓).

  1 Her son is *extremely* / *fairly* hungry. (↑)

  2 His wife is *really* / *not very* tall. (↓)

  3 Meg is *quite* / *extremely* sleepy. (↓)

  4 Ian feels *really* / *quite* bored. (↕)

  5 My brother is *extremely* / *fairly* unhappy. (↓)

LANGUAGE FOCUS Describing people

To ask about someone's personality we ask the question *What + to be + like*.

  A: *What**'s** she **like**?*

  B: *She's very friendly and kind.*

To ask about someone's looks, we ask the question *What + do + look like*.

  A: *What **does** he **look like**?*

  B: *He's quite tall and has dark hair.*

If someone is *too old*, they are older than they want to be.

  A: *Do you want to play football?*

  B: *No, thanks. I'm **too old** to play football!*

If someone is *not old enough*, they are less old than they want to be.

  *I want to go but I'm **not old enough**. You have to be over eighteen years old.*

We use *kind of* and *sort of* to describe something or someone in a general way, or when we don't need (or want) to be exact.

  *She's **kind of** quiet, but very clever.*

We usually use *a bit* to express a negative opinion.

  *Don't you think that's **a bit** selfish?*
  *He seems **a bit** unfriendly, but perhaps it's because he's shy.*

EXERCISE

1 Choose the correct options to complete the sentences.

  1 The new woman at work is *kind of* / *at all* shy but very friendly.

  2 She thinks she's not *clever enough* / *enough clever* to go to university.

  3 A: What *does she look like* / *is she like*?
    B: She's easy-going, honest … perfect for the job!

  4 Unfortunately Mark's *not very* / *a bit* talkative. We need someone quiet to work in the library.

  5 They say he's *too* / *enough* short for the basketball team. But he's a very good player.

Grammar summary | UNIT 9

GRAMMAR Past simple

Form

Affirmative	Negative
(regular) He **travelled** by dog sled.	He **didn't travel** by plane.
(irregular) We **flew** to France.	We **didn't fly** to Spain.

Question	Short answer
Did he **fly** to France?	Yes, he **did**. No, he **didn't**.

For most regular verbs we add -ed (but see spelling rules below).

> The journey **lasted** three weeks.

Notice we use the infinitive of the main verb in the negative.

> The journey **didn't last** three weeks.

Spelling rules for regular verbs

Verbs ending in -e add -d:

> arrive → arrived

Two-syllable verbs ending in -y change y to i and add -ed:

> hurry → hurried

Many verbs ending in vowel + consonant double the consonant:

> travel → travelled

Irregular verbs

Many common verbs have an irregular form, which you need to learn (e.g. come → came, eat → ate, meet → met, be → was/were).

> They **became** the first women to cross the Antarctic on foot.
> Ann Bancroft and Liv Arnesen **were** once school teachers.

For a full list of common irregular verbs, see page 166.

Use

We use the simple past to talk about completed actions in the past.

> I **worked** late last night.
> She **went** to Peru in 2014.

EXERCISES

1 Complete the sentences. Use the past tense of the verbs.

  1 I _____ (walk) for ten miles.
  2 She _____ (climb) the mountain.

3 We _____ (explore) the island.
4 They _____ (not see) the storm.
5 He _____ (not go) alone.
6 I _____ (not travel) at night.
7 He _____ (get) to the top quickly.
8 She _____ (go) skiing last month.

2 Make yes/no questions from these statements.

  1 Valentina Tereshkova became the first woman to travel in space.
    Did Valentina Tereshkova become the first woman to travel in space?
  2 Jessica Watson sailed alone around the world.
  3 Gennady Padalka broke the record for the longest time in space.
  4 Robert Ballard found the *Titanic*.
  5 Roald Amundsen's expedition got to the South Pole before Robert Scott's.
  6 Felicity Aston made the first solo journey on skis across the Antarctic.

LANGUAGE FOCUS Talking about the past

Wh- questions about the past also use the auxiliary *did*.

> When **did** they arrive?
> How long **did** the journey take?

In questions and short answers with *to be*, we use *was* and *were* and not the auxiliary *did*.

> A: **Were** they the first people to explore Australia?
> B: *Yes, they **were**. / No, they **weren't**.*
> A: **Was** she the only woman on the team?
> B: *Yes, she **was**. / No, she **wasn't**.*
> A: *Who **was** Charles Blondin?*
> B: *He **was** the first person to cross the Niagara Falls on a tightrope!*

EXERCISE

1 Complete the question for each answer.

  1 Who _____?
    Nellie Bly was a journalist and an explorer.
  2 _____ English?
    No, she was American.
  3 What _____ in 1889?
    She travelled around the world.
  4 How _____?
    She travelled by ship, train and on horseback.
  5 Where _____?
    She started her journey in New Jersey, USA.
  6 How long _____?
    Her journey took 72 days, 6 hours, 11 minutes and 6 seconds.

GRAMMAR *should* and *shouldn't*

Form

You **should** *move to a new apartment.*
You **shouldn't** *stay in your current place.*

Should *we live in the city centre?*
Yes, we **should**. */ No, we* **shouldn't**.

What time **should** *we leave for the airport?*
We **should** *leave at 4.15.*

Use

We use *should* to:

• say what is important for you to do.
   I **should** *go. I* **shouldn't** *stay.*

• give advice to others.
   You **should** *move. You* **shouldn't** *stay here.*

Notice we use the infinitive without *to* after *should* and that questions are formed without the auxiliary *do*.

EXERCISE

1 Choose the correct options to complete the text.

My neighbourhood is great. There's a lovely park where you ¹*should / can* go running and walking. My husband says I ²*should / can* run more but I prefer walking! You ³*can / should* walk safely at night because there is street lighting and very little crime. But you ⁴*do / should* always carry a phone, just in case. The only problem is that you ⁵*can't / shouldn't* get a bus to work because there is no bus service. You ⁶*shouldn't / can't* drive though – get a bike instead. There are good cycle lanes and it keeps you healthy!

LANGUAGE FOCUS Making suggestions

We can use different ways to make suggestions. *Let's, could, can* and *why don't (you)* are all used with the infinitive without *to*.

Let's *move to the countryside.*
We could *buy a small cottage.*
Maybe we can *find somewhere with a lovely garden.*
One thing we could do is *look online.*
Why don't we *ask Roy? He sells houses.*

We can also use *how about + ing.*
How about *visit**ing** a few houses this weekend?*

Notice this can mean I suggest *you* go or I suggest *we* go together. It depends on the context.

EXERCISE

1 Complete the suggestions (1–6) with the correct form of these verbs. Then match with sentences a–f.

go	have	invite	paint	try	walk

1 Let's _____ to the jazz festival in the park.
2 We could _____ the Thai restaurant that opened last week.
3 One thing we could do is _____ the bedroom.
4 Why don't we _____ around the neighbourhood for an hour or two?
5 How about _____ the neighbours for a cup of tea on Sunday?
6 Or maybe we can just _____ a nice quiet weekend for once!

a I read a good review of it.
b I'm really tired!
c I want to get to know our new area.
d I'd like to be friendly to them.
e I think it starts on Saturday.
f We never have time to do jobs in the house during the week.

GRAMMAR *look* and *look like*

Form and use

We use *look* with adjectives.
*The landscape **looks** beautiful!*

We use *look like* with nouns.
*It **looks like** a beautiful place!*

EXERCISE

1 Correct this text. ~~Cross out~~ *like* where it is incorrect.

These are some photos of when we went to South Africa and climbed Table Mountain. It really does ¹**look like** a table. When we left home, it ²**looked like** sunny and felt hot, but when we reached the top it was really cold. It was a hard climb but the views are amazing – the sea and the city ³**looked like** very beautiful from the top of the mountain. You can also see Lion's Head mountain. It doesn't really ⁴**look like** a lion's head but some people say it does from the sea. We took lots of photos. I don't like this picture of me. I ⁵**look like** weird and my face ⁶**looks like** a tomato!

LANGUAGE FOCUS Asking for and giving opinions

We can ask different questions to find out someone's opinion.

For a *yes/no* answer, we can ask:
A: **Do you think** *this is interesting?*
B: *Yes, I do. / No, I don't.*

To find out more information, we can ask:
What do you think of *this?*
How do you feel about *this?*
What's your opinion of *this?* (more formal)

To give your opinion, we can say:
I think (that) *it's boring.*
I find *it interesting.*
*It **seems** weird.*

To emphasize it's our personal opinion, we can say:
To me, *it's not very interesting.*
In my opinion, *it's her best work.* (more formal)

EXERCISE

1 Complete the questions and answers.

1 A: What do you think _____ this style of photography?
   B: I find _____ really interesting.

2 A: What's your opinion _____ this exhibition?
   B: I _____ it's fantastic – perhaps his best one.

3 A: How do you feel _____ landscape photography?
   B: _____ me, it seems less interesting than wildlife photography.

4 A: _____ you think this magazine is attractive?
   B: Not really. _____ my opinion, it's not very well designed.

GRAMMAR Zero conditional

Form

*I can't sleep **if/when** I drink too much coffee.*

***If/When** I drink too much coffee, I can't sleep.*

*Do you skip your shower **if/when** there is no hot water?*

*What do you do **if/when** you don't have any toothpaste?*

Use

You can use the zero conditional with *if* or *when* to talk about:
- scientific facts.
  ***If** you heat water to 100°C, it boils.*
- things that are always true or that you always do.
  ***When** I wash my hands, I always use soap.*

Both clauses are usually in the present simple. If you begin a sentence with *if* or *when*, add a comma.
*I wash with shampoo **if** I don't have soap.*
***If** I don't have soap, I wash with shampoo.*

EXERCISE

1 Use the zero conditional to make sentences.

1 you drink sugary drinks / it damages your teeth (if)

_____
_____

2 your breath is fresher / you clean your teeth regularly (when)

_____
_____

3 you eat a healthy breakfast / you have energy all morning (when)

_____
_____

4 you can live longer and have fewer diseases / you exercise several times a week (if)

_____
_____

5 you are happy and have good friends / it helps to protect you from heart attacks (if)

_____
_____

6 you get tired and have headaches / you don't drink enough water (when)

_____
_____

LANGUAGE FOCUS Talking about facts

To emphasize that something happens regularly we can use *every time* or *whenever*.
***Every time** I go abroad, I take hand sanitizer with me.*
***Whenever** I have five minutes free in the day, I close my eyes and relax.*

To ask what happens in particular situations you can use *if* or *when* in a question.
*What happens **if** you eat old or dirty food?*
***When** you get home from work, do you cook a healthy meal?*

EXERCISE

1 Match the two halves of the sentences.

1 Whenever I eat fruit and vegetables,
2 Every time I touch money,
3 If you give young children healthy food,
4 When I eat well and take regular exercise,
5 I buy organic fruit and vegetables
6 I feel better

a they learn good eating habits.
b whenever I can get them.
c I wash them first.
d every time I go out for a run.
e I wash my hands.
f I feel healthier.

Communication activities

Unit 3.5 **Exercise 3, page 38**

STUDENT A

1 The sentences below describe one of the jobs on page 38. Read the sentences to your partner. After each sentence, your partner can have one guess about what the job is. Your partner will score points depending on how quickly he or she can guess.

   1 I usually work inside. (5 points for a correct guess after this sentence)

   2 I don't usually work long hours. (4 points)

   3 I often work alone. (3 points)

   4 I need to be creative. (2 points)

   5 I often use a guitar or piano. (1 point)

   (Answer – Songwriter)

2 Now listen to your partner's sentences. Try to guess the job.

Unit 9.2 **Exercise 10, page 97**

STUDENT B

You and Student A have the same story. Read the story and write questions to ask for the missing information. Then take turns asking questions to complete the story.

   2 How _____ in the South Pacific?

   4 How many times _____ ?

   6 Where _____ ?

   8 What _____ ?

Australian Jessica Watson sailed around the world alone. She left Sydney on October 18, 2009. She was just 16 years old. She travelled across the South Pacific. Conditions there were not very dangerous. There were few storms, and she spent her time [2]_____ .

She then sailed across the Atlantic Ocean around South America. The Atlantic Ocean was very dangerous. During one storm, her boat rolled over [4]_____ times.

The halfway point of her journey was on January 25, 2010. It was her 100th day at sea. Jessica sailed past southern Africa and across the Indian Ocean.

On May 15, 2010, she arrived [6]_____ after a journey of 210 days. Thousands of fans greeted her. How did she feel at the end? 'I wanted to keep going', she wrote on her blog. She received [8]_____ for her achievement. She was named Young Australian of the Year in 2011.

Unit 7.2 Exercise 9, page 77

STUDENT B

Take turns to read the questions and the three options to your partner. Circle the answer they think is correct. At the end, tell them how many correct answers they got. (Correct answers are in **bold**.)

1 Death Valley is the lowest point in which country?

  a Egypt   b China   c **the United States**

2 The Gobi Desert covers almost 1.3 million square kilometres. Which one of these deserts is smaller?

  a the Sahara   b **the Atacama**   c the Arabian

3 These are all called seas, but they're really lakes. Which is the largest?

  a **the Caspian Sea**   b the Aral Sea   c the Dead Sea

4 The deepest spot on Earth is in which ocean?

  a the Atlantic   b the Indian   c **the Pacific**

5 What is the biggest island in the world?

  a Madagascar   b **Greenland**   c New Guinea

Unit 6.2 Exercise 9, page 65

STUDENT A

These are exercises you can do before an exam to help reduce stress. Look at the pictures and read the text. Take turns to cover your text and explain to your partner how to do each exercise.

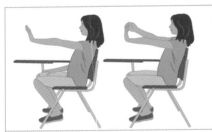  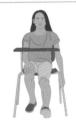

Wrist exercises	**Shoulder exercises**	**Leg and foot exercises**
Straighten your left arm and point your fingers up. Then, with your right hand, pull back on your left-hand fingers gently and hold. Repeat with your other hand.	First, lift both of your shoulders slowly to your ears. Don't move, and hold. After three seconds, relax your shoulders. Repeat five times.	Before you begin, turn slightly in your chair. Stretch your left leg out. Then move your foot in circles. Do this for fifteen seconds. Then repeat with your right leg.

This exercise is for your wrists. First, straighten your left arm and point your fingers up.

Like this?

Unit 4.5 Exercises 1–4, page 50

INTERVIEW QUESTIONS

1 Are you good with animals?

2 Are you good at maths?

3 Are you good at talking to people?

4 Can you write well?

5 Can you make people laugh easily?

6 Are you interested in fashion?

7 Are you good at swimming?

8 Are you good at giving presentations?

9 Can you sing and/or dance?

10 Are you good at making things?

11 Are you good at taking photos?

12 Are you good at giving advice?

13 Can you play a musical instrument?

14 Are you good at cooking?

15 Do you know how to speak a foreign language?

JOB VACANCIES		
Birthday party clown Dress up like a clown and entertain at kids' parties.	**Wedding planner** Plan weddings for busy couples.	**Theme park character** Dress up like a cartoon character or celebrity.
Swimming pool lifeguard Keep swimmers safe at a local public swimming pool.	**Maths teacher** Teach maths at a local school.	**Underwater photographer** Take photos of underwater animals.
Museum tour guide Guide visitors and give presentations.	**Horse trainer** Help riders train their horse.	**Summer school cooking teacher** Teach foreign visitors how to cook local food.
Food blogger Review and write about today's coolest restaurants.	**Celebrity clothes buyer** Look for and buy clothes for your celebrity boss.	**Pet shop** Help care for animals and take money from customers.
Video game designer Create and program new video games.	**Tourist office assistant** Answer questions and help tourists.	**Cruise ship entertainer** Sing and dance to entertain passengers.

Unit 10.2 Exercise 10, page 109

STUDENT A

1 Read the information. Tell Student B what kind of area you want to live in. Listen to Student B's recommendations.

> You are a student. You'd like a quiet neighbourhood and affordable housing. You want to live near the university. It would be nice to have some green space or a park nearby.

2 Listen to what Student B wants. Recommend an area in your city (or a city near you) that would be good for Student A. Give reasons for your recommendation.

Unit 3.5 Exercise 3, page 38

STUDENT B

1 Your partner will read five sentences that describe one of the jobs on page 38. After each sentence, you can have one guess about what the job is. You will score points depending on how quickly you can guess.

2 The sentences below describe one of the jobs on page 38. Read the sentences to your partner. After each sentence, your partner can have one guess about what the job is. Your partner will score points depending on how quickly he or she can guess.

 1 I sometimes work long hours. (5 points for a correct guess after this sentence)

 2 I work as part of a team. (4 points)

 3 I sometimes work inside, and sometimes outside. (3 points)

 4 A lot of people would like my job. (2 points)

 5 Many people eat popcorn when they watch me. (1 point)

(Answer – Film actor)

Unit 9.2 Exercise 10, page 97

STUDENT A

You and Student B have the same story. Read the story and write questions to ask for the missing information. Then take turns asking questions to complete the story.

 1 Where _____?

 3 What _____ like?

 5 When _____?

 7 Who _____?

Australian Jessica Watson sailed around the world alone. She left Sydney on October 18, 2009. She was just 16 years old. She travelled across [1]_____. Conditions there were not very dangerous. There were few storms, and she spent her time reading and doing her schoolwork.

She then sailed across the Atlantic Ocean around South America. The Atlantic Ocean was very [3]_____. During one storm, her boat rolled over four times.

The halfway point of her journey was [5]_____. It was her 100th day at sea. Jessica sailed past southern Africa and across the Indian Ocean.

On May 15, 2010, she arrived in Sydney Harbour after a journey of 210 days. [7]_____ greeted her. How did she feel at the end? 'I wanted to keep going', she wrote on her blog. She received a medal for her achievement. She was named Young Australian of the Year in 2011.

STUDENT A

Take turns to read the questions and the three options to your partner. Circle the answer they think is correct. At the end, tell them how many correct answers they got. (Correct answers are in **bold**.)

1 Where is the world's highest mountain outside Asia?

    a **Argentina**   b Switzerland   c Kenya

2 What is the world's largest archipelago – or group of islands?

    a Canary Islands   b French Polynesia   c **Indonesia**

3 Which one of these islands is bigger than Iceland?

    a Bali   b Easter Island   c **Cuba**

4 Which US state is the furthest south?

    a Florida   b **Hawaii**   c Texas

5 Which of these oceans is the largest?

    a **the Indian Ocean**   b the Southern Ocean   c the Arctic Ocean

STUDENT B

These are exercises you can do before an exam to help reduce stress. Look at the pictures and read the text. Take turns to cover your text and explain to your partner how to do each exercise.

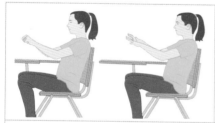

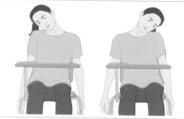

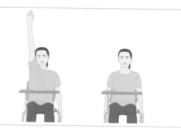

Hand exercises
First, make a tight ball with both hands. Hold for two seconds. Next, open your hands quickly and stretch your fingers out. Repeat eight times.

Neck exercises
Touch your right ear to your right shoulder. Hold for five seconds. Then touch your left ear to your left shoulder. Hold for five seconds. Repeat five times.

Arm exercises
Raise your right arm. When you cannot lift it any higher, relax and bring your arm down. Lift it again, trying to reach as high as you can. Do five times. Then repeat with your left arm.

This exercise is for your hands. First, make a tight ball with your hands.

Like this?

NEIGHBOURHOOD MAP

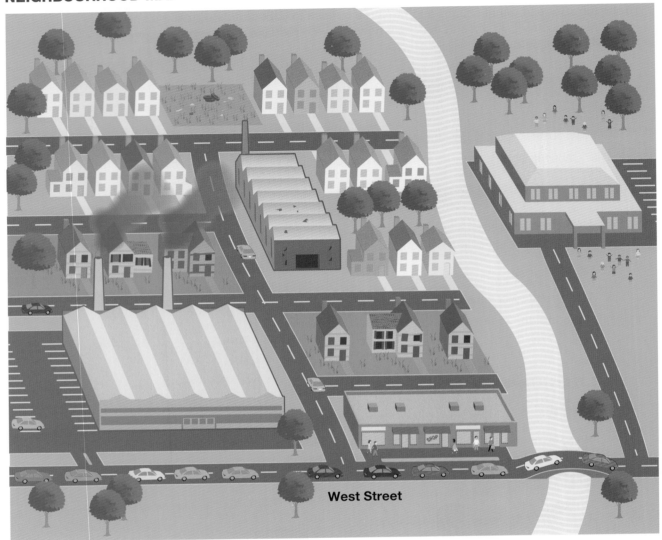

West Street

Look at the map. Decide which of the problems below you think this neighbourhood has.
Can you see any other problems?

- There are not enough parks.
- There are a lot of empty buildings.
- The traffic on West Street is very heavy.
- It takes a long time for children to get to school from their homes.
- The air quality is poor.
- There is very little entertainment.
- There aren't enough shops.
- There is no public transport.

Unit 11.2 Exercise 11, page 119

Unit 12.5 Exercise 2, page 134

A food hygiene quiz

1 **Myth.** 'Best before' dates are used to show when food is best to eat. Most food is still safe to eat after the 'best before' date. However, don't eat food after the 'use by' date!

2 **Myth.** As soon as food touches the floor, it picks up germs.

3 **Myth.** There's no difference between wooden and plastic cutting boards. Whichever you use, it needs to be clean.

4 **Myth.** Germs are easily spread by the water as you wash the chicken. Cooking the chicken properly kills any any germs.

5 **Fact.** Any germs are on the outside of a steak. So if you cook the outside it's safe to eat.

6 **Myth.** Most burgers are made from chopped meat. This means that germs could be on the inside. It's important to cook the middle of any burger.

7 **Fact.** This is to stop germs from uncooked food dripping down onto cooked food.

Unit 10.2 Exercise 10, page 109

STUDENT B

1 Listen to what Student A wants. Recommend an area in your city (or a city near you) that you think would be good for Student A. Give reasons for your recommendation.

2 Read the information below. Tell Student A what kind of area you want to live in. Listen to Student A's recommendations.

> You just started a job in the city, so you'd like to live in a fun neighbourhood close to the centre with good public transport. You want to be close to nice cafés and restaurants.

Audioscripts

Unit 1

▶ **1.2**

Hi, my name's Philip and I'm from Oldham, a town in the north of England.

My passion in life is music. I love listening to music but I also like writing and recording my own songs.

I have quite a big collection of musical instruments: a bass guitar [music]; a mandolin [music]; a ukulele [music]; an acoustic guitar [music]; and four electric guitars. This one is my favourite.

I don't have a favourite kind of music. I like rock, country, jazz, classical – anything that's good really.

Right now, I'm a member of an Irish folk band. I play the bass guitar and mandolin. We usually play traditional Irish folk. Here, let me give you an example. [music]

▶ **1.5**

A: Hey, this chart is pretty interesting. Look.

B: Yeah? What does it show?

A: Well, it shows how popular different types of music are with different age groups. Look, you can see that classical music is popular with people over 55.

B: Well, my grandmother's a bit different. She doesn't like classical music at all. She loves pop.

A: Pop? Really?

B: Yeah. Her favourite band is One Direction.

A: Wow! That's cool. Well, what kind of music do you like? You're 20. The chart says rap and hip-hop are popular with your age group.

B: Well, that's kind of right. I like rap and hip hop. But I really love pop. I guess I'm similar to my grandmother.

Unit 2

▶ **2.1**

Well, I love live music so I spend a lot of money going to concerts and music festivals. I go to a concert maybe once a month. Tickets are sometimes very expensive for these events, but it's a bit of a passion of mine.

Also, I like fashion and clothes shopping. I love going to markets especially. I don't buy expensive clothes but I probably buy something new most weekends so I suppose, yes, over a year, I spend quite a lot.

I think it's OK though because there are other things I don't spend much on. Some of my friends go to restaurants a lot, but I love cooking so I don't often eat out and eating at home isn't expensive. I don't spend much on my mobile phone either. I prefer to sit and talk to friends face-to-face and I never use my phone to download films or music.

▶ **2.5**

A: Hey, look at this chart. It says that the average teenager spends 29 per cent of their money on clothes!

B: Hmm. Well that's probably true for me. I go shopping for clothes every weekend.

A: Really? Not me. I hardly ever buy new clothes.

B: So what do you spend your money on then?

A: I spend a lot on books, actually. I love reading.

B: Yeah? How often do you buy books?

A: Hmm. I buy about two or three new books every week.

B: Wow! I guess you usually buy them second-hand?

A: No, hardly ever actually. I prefer to buy new ones.

▶ **2.7**

1   Do you ever buy magazines?

2   Do you ever shop online?

3   How often do you spend money on clothes?

4   How often do you buy new shoes?

Unit 3

▶ **3.2**

I = Interviewer, R = Richard Lenton

I: So, Richard, can you tell us about your job? What do you do?

R: I'm a TV host and journalist. The TV hosting part of my career has always been in sport, usually soccer. I've presented live matches in the Premier League, European Champions League, the FA Cup and World Cup, as well as international games.

I: What's the best thing about your job?

R: The best thing is that I'm working in sport – which is my life and passion. I really enjoy going to work. Working on live matches is really exciting. I've also been able to meet some famous people, including two of my biggest sporting heroes, Lennox Lewis and Ian Botham, and I've interviewed people like Usain Bolt and David Beckham.

I: Wow, cool! Is there anything you don't like about your job?

R: Well, it is sometimes tiring, especially when I need to work in the middle of the night. For example, during the World Cup in 2014, I went to work at 10pm and came home at 8am the following day. However, I would have to say that it was the best experience of my working life.

I: And what do you do in your free time, when you're not working?

R: I go to the gym nearly every day before I start work, and I play soccer at weekends. I would like to play more than one game a week, but my body simply can't handle it! I also like to travel as much as possible. There are so many interesting places to visit in this part of the world.

▶ **3.7**

A: So what do you do for a living?

B: Oh, I'm a journalist for a local newspaper.

A: Hmm. Sounds great!

B: Really? It's not actually.

A: Oh? What don't you like about it?

B: Well, the pay is OK but I really don't like the hours. They're terrible. I start work at 7am every day, and usually finish at around 8pm.

A: Wow, that's tough! So what's your dream job?

B: My dream job? Well, I think I'd really like to be a charity worker. You know, I'd love to do something to help other people.

▶ 3.18

1 I don't work in an office.

2 I meet new people every day.

3 I never work at night.

4 I always work outside.

5 I teach people how to do something.

Unit 4

▶ 4.1

Okotanpe is from Japan. He has a unique ability. Okotanpe is a contact juggler – and he's very good at it. He has many popular videos on YouTube that show his amazing skills.

Contact juggling is different to normal juggling. You don't throw the balls in the air – instead the ball always touches, and rolls around, your body.

The balls look like bubbles, but actually they are hard and made of plastic. If you're good at contact juggling, like Okotanpe, you can make the ball look like it's floating. But you need to practise a lot. Okotanpe practises for several hours every day.

Okotanpe can also do magic tricks with the balls – and he can make it look very easy.

▶ 4.6

A: Are you still thinking about changing your career?

B: I'm thinking about it, yes.

A: Oh, there are some fun jobs here! How about becoming a pearl diver?

B: A pearl diver? Haha. Well it sounds fun, but I can't swim.

A: Oh, that's a shame.

B: How about you? You're good at swimming.

A: Yeah, but I can't swim underwater very well.

B: I see. Are there any other jobs there?

A: How about becoming a voice artist?

B: Actually, that's not such a bad idea. I can speak in funny voices and I love acting.

A: Well, why not give it a try!

Unit 5

▶ 5.1

In 2015, Sam Cossman visited Vanuatu on a project to study an active volcano. Cossman and his team learned a lot about this amazing place. They also took some great photos and made an incredible video. To get images like these, the team used drones.

They put cameras onto the drones and flew them close to the centre of the volcano. Not all of the drones survived. Some drones crashed into the volcano and others were destroyed by the intense heat. But the team were still able to get the pictures they wanted.

The drones were really important to the success of the mission. Cossman believes that new technology is changing the way we explore.

He also used a special suit to get close to the volcano and take a look by himself. The suit can cope with temperatures of up to 1,600 degrees Celsius.

Cossman says that while the experience was 'terrifying', it also made him truly feel alive.

▶ 5.5

A: This stuff is crazy! How much wearable technology is really useful, do you think?

B: Some of it's great! I'd love some smart glasses for photos and video. I take a lot of photos. What about you?

A: Hmm. I don't use much technology. The only wearable tech I have is my fitness band.

B: Yeah? What does that do?

A: I wear it when I exercise. For example, it tells me how many kilometres I walk each day.

B: That's cool. How many kilometres do you usually do?

A: Er, not many – about six on a good day.

Unit 6

▶ 6.3

When Vasu Sojitra was about nine months old, he lost his right leg to a blood infection. But even from a young age it was clear that Sojitra wasn't going to let his condition slow him down. He enjoyed sports, such as football, and also took up skateboarding.

However, when he was ten, Sojitra found his real passion – skiing. Sojitra taught himself because the ski school instructor had no idea how to teach him.

At first it was difficult, but Sojitra just kept trying and eventually he realized he was capable of doing anything.

Sojitra likes to ski off-piste. There are no ski lifts so he needs to get to the top of the mountains himself. Although it's tiring, Sojitra loves the challenge. He always wants to hike the highest mountain and get to the top of it.

And on the way down – it's so much fun! Sojitra skis just as fast as his skiing partners.

▶ 6.6

A: How are your exams going?

B: Not bad actually. I think I'm doing pretty well.

A: I don't know how you stay so relaxed about it all. I'm really stressed.

B: Well, it's important to stay organized. I plan each day's work carefully and try to manage my time.

A: I do that too. But when I have an exam I'm so stressed I can't think properly.

B: I always listen to relaxing music before I have an exam. That keeps me calm. And then, after the exam, I reward myself by going shopping. That gives me something to look forward to.

A: That sounds like a good idea. Perhaps I'll try it.

Unit 7

▶ 7.2

Ross Donihue: Marty and I set out on an expedition to make the first print and interactive maps of Patagonia national park. This was a dream project. In Patagonia we wanted to explore as much of the park as we could.

Narrator: Patagonia is an area at the southern end of South America. It's shared by Chile and Argentina. It's a big place but only about 2 million people live there. It's usually very cool and dry. Creating a map of this place involves a lot of hiking. But the scenery makes it worthwhile.

RD: Look at that – it doesn't get much better than that – every day it's different. What I love most about Patagonia is no two days are the same, the weather's constantly changing, the light is constantly changing. You never know what the sunrise or sunset or anything in between will hold. And then we get to come back and produce a beautiful map that represents this place and, you know, share that with other people. That's really why I do it.

▶ 7.6

A: Which place in the world would you most like to visit?

B: I'd love to climb Paricutin Volcano one day.

A: Yeah? Not me. It sounds too dangerous! I heard it's the most beautiful volcano in the world though.

B: Yeah, it's really beautiful. But I don't think it's so dangerous.

A: Maybe you're right. But I'd prefer something a bit less challenging. I really want to visit the Grand Canyon.

B: Yeah, me too. I heard the Copper Canyon in Mexico is deeper, though.

A: Really? Well, maybe I could visit both.

B: Good idea!

Unit 8

▶ 8.2

Everybody says that my mum and I look very similar. My mum looks very young for her age, and sometimes people think that we're sisters. We do look quite similar I suppose. We're both quite tall, we have the same eyes and a similar smile.

Our personalities are similar, too. Neither of us are very talkative. We're both quite shy actually. And we both worry a lot – neither of us are very easy-going. But we have very different interests. My mum really likes sport, especially baseball. But I'm really not interested. And my mum enjoys cooking, but I don't like it so much. Actually my mum's a really good cook. I love the food she makes. But I also like food from different countries such as Thai food and Japanese food. My mum's a bit more traditional and usually prefers to eat Korean food.

▶ 8.5

It's interesting to see how people of different nationalities feel about their appearance. What's also really interesting is that using the same data we can also look at the differences between men and women.

Now you might think that the responses would be very different. Some people think that women have more body image issues than men – but the survey results don't really support that.

When we look at the results across all countries there is only a small difference between how men and women feel about how they look.

Twelve per cent of both men and women said they were extremely happy with the way they look.

And at the other end of the scale, fourteen per cent of women said they were not very happy with their looks. Eleven per cent of men gave the same answer. Similarly, four per cent of women said they were quite unhappy, as did three per cent of men.

Unit 9

▶ 9.2

In 2012, I set myself a challenge. I wanted to try to run twelve full-course marathons in one year. I had never run a full marathon before, so I knew it wouldn't be easy.

I like travelling so I also wanted to run in different countries. I planned to run marathons in Japan, Korean, Malaysia, Iceland and Thailand.

My first marathon was in Okinawa, Japan. On the morning of the race, I was pretty nervous. But the weather was beautiful, the atmosphere was fantastic and my training beforehand was just enough – I finished the race! It was an amazing feeling!

My favourite marathon was the one in Reykjavik, Iceland. Iceland is a beautiful country and the scenery along the course was breath-taking.

The most difficult race was in Kuala Lumpur. First of all, it was really hot. But, my biggest mistake was that I forgot to pack my running shoes! Can you believe it?! So, the day before the race, I had to buy new shoes and during the race, my feet were pretty painful!

In Gwacheon, which is in Korea, I managed to finish in third place! This was a real shock. I only realized it after the race was already over but I was very happy!

After my last race in Bangkok, I had completed my challenge. I still enjoy running. I'm currently preparing for a full marathon in Stockholm. And maybe I'll try running 20 marathons in 2020!

▶ 9.5

Ann Bancroft and Liv Arnesen were once school teachers. But in February 2001, they became the first women to cross the Antarctic on foot. They walked, skied and ice-sailed for more than 2,700 kilometres in extremely cold and dangerous conditions. The journey lasted three months. Bancroft and Arnesen wanted their adventure to inspire others to their own achievements. Using a website and satellite phone calls, more than three million children from around the world were able to watch and share in this amazing journey.

Unit 10

▶ 10.2

I'm from South Africa. I grew up in a city called Pietermaritzburg. It's in the west of the country, not so far from Durban.

I grew up in a quiet neighbourhood in the suburbs. It's a really nice place with a lot of nature and green space. There are a lot of fruit trees around, and as children we used to pick the fruit and hang out and eat it all day.

Traffic isn't so heavy, so the children can play in the streets. I spent a lot of time outside when I was young.

There's a university in Pietermaritzburg, so the nightlife is pretty good near the city centre.

The only downside I guess is that in my neighbourhood the public transportation isn't very good. So it's a bit difficult to get around if you don't have a car.

But it was a really good place to grow up. I think I was pretty lucky to live there.

▶ 10.5

A: So where should we move to? We shouldn't leave it much longer.

B: I agree. We need to start looking. Well, how about Brentwood? It's a beautiful area – there are lots of parks and green space.

A: Yeah, but it's too far from the office for me. What about Crestview instead? I know some great restaurants there.

B: Crestview? No thanks, it's much too noisy.

A: OK. Well, we should think about Woodlands. It's pretty green and it's not so far from work.

B: Yeah. That's not a bad idea. Why don't we go for a look around the neighbourhood this weekend?

Unit 11

▶ 11.1

Hi, my name's Hannah. I'm a documentary and travel photographer from the Philippines. Photography is a great passion of mine and I'm really lucky that my job is something that I love.

People sometimes ask me about what's important when taking a photo. Well, to me, the most important thing is making sure you are in the right place to take the photograph. But this doesn't mean that you have to be very somewhere very far from home. Sometimes the right place can just be in your back yard, your school, or your neighbourhood.

Of course there are also technical things that a good photographer needs to learn. As a photographer you need to make sure you learn how to observe light. You need to be able to understand how different times of day make for different kinds of images. My favourite time to take photographs is right before sundown, when the light is very soft.

This is one of my favourite photos. I took it when I was in Batanes, an island in the Philippines, photographing indigenous cultures. I like the perspective and the colour. But also, I like it because it shows how lovely my country is, and it reminds me of the wonders of childhood, when everything felt like a giant playground.

▶ 11.6

A: Look at this picture. Do you think it's real?

B: Wow. It looks real. But I've never seen a sink that big!

A: Yeah. Look at the lighting. To me, something isn't quite right.

B: I think you're right. And look at the boy's shadow – I think it's going in the wrong direction.

A: Oh yeah. That looks a bit weird. OK, I think this is definitely not real.

Unit 12

▶ 12.1

I have a problem with coffee I think. I drink way too much of it. When I'm at work, I'd say I drink at least five or six cups a day. It's become a habit, I guess, and the problem is that if I don't drink coffee during the day, I start to feel really tired.

I think it has an effect on my sleep, too. I almost never get eight hours of sleep. Usually I get five or six hours of sleep, and of course the next day I feel tired, and I drink more coffee and, well, you get the picture.

But otherwise I'm really healthy. I never eat snacks between meals, I take vitamins every day and I rarely get sick. I also do quite a lot of exercise. I ride a bike, I play soccer sometimes, so I keep pretty fit.

I have a few other bad habits too, but I'm not going to tell you about those!

▶ 12.5

Most people know that washing your hands with soap is important to help prevent the spread of diseases. However, not many people consider hand-drying.

After I wash my hands, I always use a paper towel (if there is one). Let me tell you why. Even after washing your hands, there are still some germs left on them. If you don't dry your hands at all, germs can spread very easily when you touch things.

The problem with a warm-air dryer is that it may not make your hands completely dry. A jet-air dryer can dry your hands quite well, but they can also blow the germs off your hands and spread them around the bathroom.

So, a simple paper towel is much more hygienic. When you use a paper towel, germs don't get blown around and your hands will be nice and dry.

TED Talk transcripts

The transcripts use British English for all the talks, irrespective of the nationality of the speaker.

Any grammatical inaccuracies in the talks have been left uncorrected in the transcripts.

Unit 1 Sleepy Man Banjo Boys: Bluegrass virtuosity from … New Jersey?

Robbie Mizzone: Thank you.

Tommy Mizzone: Thank you very much. We're so excited to be here. It's such an honour for us. Like he said, we're three brothers from New Jersey – you know, the bluegrass capital of the world. We discovered bluegrass a few years ago, and we fell in love with it. We hope you guys will too.

RM: I'm just going to take a second to introduce the band. On guitar is my fifteen-year-old brother Tommy. On banjo is ten-year-old Jonny. He's also our brother. And I'm Robbie, and I'm fourteen, and I play the fiddle.

[. . .] I'm also going to explain – a lot of people want to know where we got the name Sleepy Man Banjo Boys from. So it started when Jonny was little, and he first started the banjo, he would play on his back with his eyes closed, and we'd say it looked like he was sleeping.

[Music]

TM: Thank you very much.

RM: Thank you.

Unit 2 Jessi Arrington: Wearing nothing new

Part 1

I'm Jessi, and this is my suitcase. But before I show you what I've got inside, I'm going to make a very public confession, and that is, I'm outfit-obsessed. I love finding, wearing – and more recently – photographing and blogging a different, colourful, crazy outfit for every single occasion. But I don't buy anything new. I get all my clothes second-hand from flea markets and thrift stores. Aww, thank you. Second-hand shopping allows me to reduce the impact my wardrobe has on the environment and on my wallet. I get to meet all kinds of great people; my dollars usually go to a good cause; I look pretty unique; and it makes shopping like my own personal treasure hunt. I mean, what am I going to find today? Is it going to be my size? Will I like the colour? Will it be under $20? If all the answers are 'yes', I feel as though I've won.

Part 2

And I'd really love to show you my week's worth of outfits right now. Does that sound good?

So as I do this, I'm also going to tell you a few of the life lessons that, believe it or not, I have picked up in these adventures wearing nothing new. So let's start with Sunday. I call this 'Shiny Tiger'. You do not have to spend a lot of money to look great. You can almost always look phenomenal for under $50.

[. . .] Monday: Colour is powerful. It is almost physiologically impossible to be in a bad mood when you're wearing bright red pants. [Laughter] If you are happy, you are going to attract other happy people to you.

Tuesday: Fitting in is way overrated. I've spent a whole lot of my life trying to be myself and at the same time fit in. Just be who you are.

[. . .] Wednesday: Embrace your inner child. Sometimes people tell me that I look like I'm playing dress-up, or that I remind them of their seven-year-old. I like to smile and say, 'Thank you'.

Thursday: Confidence is key. If you think you look good in something, you almost certainly do. And if you don't think you look good in something, you're also probably right.

[. . .] Friday: A universal truth – five words for you: Gold sequins go with everything.

And finally, Saturday: Developing your own unique personal style is a really great way to tell the world something about you without having to say a word. It's been proven to me time and time again as people have walked up to me this week simply because of what I'm wearing, and we've had great conversations.

So obviously this is not all going to fit back in my tiny suitcase. So before I go home to Brooklyn, I'm going to donate everything back. Because the lesson I'm trying to learn myself this week is that it's OK to let go. I don't need to get emotionally attached to these things because around the corner, there is always going to be another crazy, colourful, shiny outfit just waiting for me, if I put a little love in my heart and look.

Thank you very much. Thank you.

Unit 3 Chris Burkard: The joy of surfing in ice-cold water

Part 1

So if I told you that this was the face of pure joy, would you call me crazy? I wouldn't blame you, because every time I look at this Arctic selfie, I shiver just a little bit. I want to tell you a little bit about this photograph.

I was swimming around in the Lofoten Islands in Norway, just inside the Arctic Circle, and the water was hovering right at freezing.

[. . .] Now, before we get into the why would anyone ever want to surf in freezing cold water, I would love to give you a little perspective on what a day in my life can look like.

[Video] Man: I mean, I know we were hoping for good waves, but I don't think anybody thought that was going to happen. I can't stop shaking. I'm so cold.

Part 2

So, surf photographer, right? I don't even know if it's a real job title, to be honest. My parents definitely didn't think so when I told them at nineteen I was quitting my job to pursue this dream career: blue skies, warm tropical beaches and a tan that lasts all year long. I mean, to me, this was it. Life could not get any better. Sweating it out, shooting surfers in these exotic tourist destinations. But there was just this one problem. You see, the more time I spent travelling to these exotic locations, the less gratifying it seemed to be. I set out seeking adventure, and what I was finding was only routine.

[. . .] There's only about a third of the Earth's oceans that are warm, and it's really just that thin band around the equator. So if I was going to find perfect waves, it was probably going to happen somewhere cold, where the seas are notoriously rough, and that's exactly where I began to look. And it was my first trip to Iceland that I felt like I found exactly what I was looking for.

I was blown away by the natural beauty of the landscape, but most importantly, I couldn't believe we were finding perfect waves in such a remote and rugged part of the world.

[. . .] And I realized, all this shivering had actually taught me something: in life, there are no shortcuts to joy. Anything that is worth pursuing is going to require us to suffer just a little bit, and that tiny bit of suffering that I did for my photography, it added a value to my work that was so much more meaningful to me than just trying to fill the pages of magazines.

[. . .] So I look back at this photograph. It's easy to see frozen fingers and cold wet suits and even the struggle that it took just to get there, but most of all, what I see is just joy.

Thank you so much.

Unit 4 Tom Thum: The orchestra in my mouth

Part 1

We're going to take it back, way back, back into time. [Beatboxing: 'Billie Jean']

[Applause] All right. Wassup. Thank you very much, TEDx.

If you guys haven't figured it out already, my name's Tom Thum and I'm a beatboxer, which means all the sounds that you just heard were made entirely using just my voice, and the only thing was my voice. And I can assure you there are absolutely no effects on this microphone whatsoever.

And I'm very, very stoked – you guys are just applauding for everything. It's great. Look at this, Mum! I made it!

[. . .] You know, I'm from Brisbane, which is a great city to live in. Yeah! All right! Most of Brisbane's here. That's good. You know, I'm from Brissy, which is a great city to live in, but let's be honest – it's not exactly the cultural hub of the Southern Hemisphere. So I do a lot of my work outside Brisbane and outside Australia, and so the pursuit of this crazy passion of mine has enabled me to see so many amazing places in the world.

Part 2

I would like to share with you some technology that I brought all the way from the thriving metropolis of Brisbane. These things in front of me here are called Kaoss Pads, and they allow me to do a whole lot of different things with my voice. For example, the one on the left here allows me to add a little bit of reverb to my sound, which gives me that – [Trumpet] – flavour. [Laughter] And the other ones here, I can use them in unison to mimic the effect of a drum machine or something like that. I can sample in my own sounds and I can play it back just by hitting the pads here. [Applause]

I've got way too much time on my hands. And last but not least, the one on my right here allows me to loop loop loop loop loop loop loop loop my voice.

Part 3

So with all that in mind, ladies and gentlemen, I would like to take you on a journey to a completely separate part of

Earth as I transform the Sydney Opera House into a smoky downtown jazz bar. All right boys, take it away. [Music]

Ladies and gentlemen, I'd like to introduce you to a very special friend of mine, one of the greatest double bassists I know. Mr Smokey Jefferson, let's take it for a walk. Come on, baby. [Music]

All right, ladies and gentlemen, I'd like to introduce you to the star of the show, one of the greatest jazz legends of our time. Music lovers and jazz lovers alike, please give a warm hand of applause for the one and only Mr Peeping Tom. Take it away. [Music] [Applause]

Thank you. Thank you very much.

Unit 5 Yves Rossy: Fly with the Jetman

Part 1

Narrator: Many of the tests are conducted while Yves is strapped into the wing, because Yves' body is an integral part of the aircraft. The wing has no steering controls, no flaps, no rudder. Yves uses his body to steer the wing. When he arches his back, he gains altitude. When he pushes his shoulders forward, he goes into a dive.

[. . .] Commentator One: There he goes. There is Yves Rossy. And I think the wing is open. So our first critical moment, it's open. He is down. Is he flying?

Commentator Two: It looks like he's stabilized. He's starting to make his climb.

Commentator One: There's that 90 degree turn you're talking about, taking him out over the channel. There is Yves Rossy. There is no turning back now. He is over the English Channel and under way. Ladies and gentlemen, a historic flight has begun.

[. . .] Commentator One: There he is. Yves Rossy has landed in England.

Bruno Giussani: And now he's in Edinburgh. Yves Rossy! [Applause]

Part 2

[What's it like up there?]

Yves Rossy: It's fun. It's fun. I don't have feathers. But I feel like a bird sometimes. It's really an unreal feeling, because normally you have a big thing, a plane, around you. And when I strap just this little harness, this little wing, I really have the feeling of being a bird.

[How did you become Jetman?]

YR: It was about 20 years ago, when I discovered free falling. When you go out of an airplane, you are almost naked. You take a position like that. And especially when you take a tracking position, you have the feeling that you are flying. And that's the nearest thing to the dream. You have no machine around you. You are just in the element. It's very short and only in one direction.

[What's your top speed?]

YR: It's about 300 kilometres per hour before looping. That means about 190 miles per hour.

[What's the weight of your equipment?]

YR: When I exit full of kerosene, I'm about 55 kilos. I have 55 kilos on my back.

[What's next for Jetman?]

YR: First, to instruct a younger guy. I want to share it, to do formation flights. And I plan to start from a cliff, like catapulted from a cliff.

BG: So instead of jumping off a plane, yes?

YR: Yes, with the final goal to take off, but with initial speed. Really, I go step by step. It seems a little bit crazy, but it's not. It's possible to start already now, it's just too dangerous. Thanks to the increasing technology, better technology, it will be safe. And I hope it will be for everybody.

BG: Yves, thank you very much. Yves Rossy.

Unit 6 Daniel Kish: How I use sonar to navigate the world

Part 1

[Clicking]

[. . .] Many of you may have heard me clicking as I came onto the stage – [clicking] – with my tongue. Those are flashes of sound that go out and reflect from surfaces all around me, just like a bat's sonar, and return to me with patterns, with pieces of information, much as light does for you. And my brain, thanks to my parents, has been activated to form images in my visual cortex, which we now call the imaging system, from those patterns of information, much as your brain does. I call this process flash sonar. It is how I have learned to see through my blindness, to navigate my journey through the dark unknowns of my own challenges.

Part 2

[. . .] But I was not raised to think of myself as in any way remarkable. I have always regarded myself much like anyone else who navigates the dark unknowns of their own challenges. Is that so remarkable? I do not use my eyes; I use my brain. Now, someone, somewhere, must think that's remarkable, or I wouldn't be up here, but let's consider this for a moment.

Everyone out there who faces or who has ever faced a challenge, raise your hands. Whoosh. OK. Lots of hands going up, a moment, let me do a head count. This will take a while. OK, lots of hands in the air. Keep them up. I have an idea. Those of you who use your brains to navigate these challenges, put your hands down. OK, anyone with your hands still up has challenges of your own.

Part 3

[. . .] So now I present to you a challenge. So if you'd all close your eyes for just a moment, OK? And you're going to learn a bit of flash sonar. I'm going to make a sound. I'm going to hold this panel in front of me, but I'm not going to move it. Just listen to the sound for a moment. Shhhhhhhhhh. OK, nothing very interesting. Now, listen to what happens to that same exact sound when I move the panel. Shhhhhhhhhh.

[. . .] OK, now keep your eyes closed because, did you hear the difference? OK. Now, let's be sure. For your challenge, you tell me, just say 'now' when you hear the panel start to move. OK? We'll relax into this. Shhhhhhhhhh.

Audience: Now.

Daniel Kish: Good. Excellent. Open your eyes. All right. So just a few centimetres, you would notice the difference. You've experienced sonar. You'd all make great blind people.

Part 4

Let's have a look at what can happen when this activation process is given some time and attention.

[Video] Juan Ruiz: It's like you guys can see with your eyes, and we can see with our ears.

Brian Bushway: It's not a matter of enjoying it more or less, it's about enjoying it differently.

Shawn Marsolais: It goes across.

DK: Yeah.

SM: And then it's gradually coming back down again.

DK: Yes!

SM: That's amazing. I can, like, see the car. Holy mother!

J. Louchart: I love being blind. If I had the opportunity, honestly, I wouldn't go back to being sighted.

JR: The bigger the goal, the more obstacles you'll face, and on the other side of that goal is victory. [In Italian]

DK: Now, do these people look terrified? Not so much. We have delivered activation training to tens of thousands of blind and sighted people from all backgrounds in nearly 40 countries. When blind people learn to see, sighted people seem inspired to want to learn to see their way better, more clearly, with less fear, because this exemplifies the immense capacity within us all to navigate any type of challenge, through any form of darkness, to discoveries unimagined when we are activated. I wish you all a most activating journey.

Thank you very much.

Unit 7 Karen Bass: Unseen footage, untamed nature

Part 1

As a filmmaker, I've been from one end of the Earth to the other trying to get the perfect shot and to capture animal behaviour never seen before. And what's more, I'm really lucky, because I get to share that with millions of people worldwide. Now the idea of having new perspectives of our planet and actually being able to get that message out gets me out of bed every day with a spring in my step.

You might think that it's quite hard to find new stories and new subjects, but new technology is changing the way we can film. It's enabling us to get fresh, new images and tell brand new stories.

[. . .] For a filmmaker, new technology is an amazing tool, but the other thing that really, really excites me is when new species are discovered. Now, when I heard about one animal, I knew we had to get it for my next series, *Untamed Americas,* for National Geographic.

Part 2

In 2005, a new species of bat was discovered in the cloud forests of Ecuador. And what was amazing about that discovery is that it also solved the mystery of what pollinated a unique flower. It depends solely on the bat.

[Video] Narrator: The tube-lipped nectar bat. A pool of delicious nectar lies at the bottom of each flower's long flute. But how to reach it? Necessity is the mother of evolution. [Music] This two-and-a-half-inch bat has a three-and-a-half-inch tongue, the longest relative to body length of any mammal in the world. If human, he'd have a nine-foot tongue.

KB: What a tongue! We filmed it by cutting a tiny little hole in the base of the flower and using a camera that could slow the action by 40 times. So imagine how quick that thing is in real life.

Part 3

Now people often ask me, 'Where's your favourite place on the planet?' And the truth is I just don't have one. There are so many wonderful places. But some locations draw you back time and time again. And one remote location – I first went there as a backpacker; I've been back several times for filming, most recently for *Untamed Americas* – it's the Altiplano in the high Andes of South America, and it's the most otherworldly place I know. But at 15,000 feet, it's tough. It's freezing cold, and that thin air really gets you. Sometimes it's hard to breathe, especially carrying all the heavy filming equipment.

[. . .] But the advantage of that wonderful thin atmosphere is that it enables you to see the stars in the heavens with amazing clarity. Have a look.

[Video] Narrator: Some 1,500 miles south of the tropics, between Chile and Bolivia, the Andes completely change. It's called the Altiplano, or 'high plains' – a place of extremes and extreme contrasts. Where deserts freeze and waters boil. More like Mars than Earth, it seems just as hostile to life. The stars themselves – at 12,000 feet, the dry, thin air makes for perfect stargazing. Some of the world's astronomers have telescopes nearby. But just looking up with the naked eye, you really don't need one.

KB: Thank you so much for letting me share some images of our magnificent, wonderful Earth. Thank you for letting me share that with you.

Unit 8 Meaghan Ramsey: Why thinking you're ugly is bad for you

Part 1

When is it suddenly not OK to love the way that we look? Because apparently we don't. Ten thousand people every month google, 'Am I ugly?'

This is Faye. Faye is thirteen, and she lives in Denver. And like any teenager, she just wants to be liked and to fit in. It's Sunday night. She's getting ready for the week ahead at school. And she's slightly dreading it, and she's a bit confused because despite her mum telling her all the time that she's beautiful, every day at school, someone tells her that she's ugly. Because of the difference between what her mum tells her and what her friends at school, or her peers at school, are telling her, she doesn't know who to believe. So, she takes a video of herself. She posts it to YouTube and she asks people to please leave a comment: 'Am I pretty or am I ugly?'

[. . .] Thousands of people are posting videos like this, mostly teenage girls, reaching out in this way. But what's leading them to do this? Well, today's teenagers are rarely alone. They're under pressure to be online and available at all times, talking, messaging, liking, commenting, sharing, posting – it never ends.

[. . .] This always-on environment is training our kids to value themselves based on the number of likes they get and the types of comments that they receive. There's no separation between online and offline life. What's real or what isn't is really hard to tell the difference between.

Part 2

Surely we want our kids to grow up as healthy, well-balanced individuals. But in an image-obsessed culture, we are training our kids to spend more time and mental effort on their appearance at the expense of all of the other aspects of their identities. So, things like their relationships, the development of their physical abilities, and their studies and so on, begin to suffer. Six out of ten girls are now choosing not to do something because they don't think they look good enough.

[. . .] Thirty-one per cent, nearly one in three teenagers, are withdrawing from classroom debate. They're failing to engage in classroom debate because they don't want to draw attention to the way that they look. One in five are not showing up to class at all on days when they don't feel good about it. And when it comes to exams, if you don't think you look good enough, specifically if you don't think you are thin enough, you will score a lower grade point average than your peers who are not concerned with this. And this is consistent across Finland, the US and China, and is true regardless of how much you actually weigh. So to be super clear, we're talking about the way you think you look, not how you actually look.

Part 3

We need to start judging people by what they do, not what they look like. We can all start by taking responsibility for the types of pictures and comments that we post on our own social networks. We can compliment people based on their effort and their actions and not on their appearance.

Ultimately, we need to work together as communities, as governments, and as businesses to really change this culture of ours so that our kids grow up valuing their whole selves, valuing individuality, diversity, inclusion. We need to put the people that are making a real difference on our pedestals, making a difference in the real world.

[. . .] Right now, our culture's obsession with image is holding us all back. But let's show our kids the truth. Let's show them that the way you look is just one part of your identity and that the truth is we love them for who they are and what they do and how they make us feel. Let's build self-esteem into our school curriculums. Let's each and every one of us change the way we talk and compare ourselves to other people. And let's work together as communities, from grassroots to governments, so that the happy little one-year-olds of today become the confident changemakers of tomorrow. Let's do this.

Unit 9 Robert Swan: Let's save the last pristine continent

Part 1

Let's go south. All of you are actually going south. This is the direction of south, this way, and if you go 8,000 kilometres out of the back of this room, you will come to as far south as you can go anywhere on Earth, the Pole itself.

Now, I am not an explorer. I'm not an environmentalist. I'm actually just a survivor, and these photographs that I'm showing you here are dangerous. They are the ice melt of the South and North Poles. And ladies and gentlemen, we need to listen to what these places are telling us, and if we don't, we will end up with our own survival situation here on planet Earth.

I have faced head-on these places, and to walk across a melting ocean of ice is without doubt the most frightening thing that ever happened to me.

[. . .] In this photograph, we are standing in an area the size of the United States of America, and we're on our own. We have no radio communications, no backup. Beneath our feet, 90 per cent of all the world's ice, 70 per cent of all the world's freshwater. We're standing on it. This is the power of Antarctica.

On this journey, we faced the danger of crevasses, intense cold, so cold that sweat turns to ice inside your clothing, your teeth can crack, water can freeze in your eyes. Let's just say it's a bit chilly. [Laughter] And after 70 desperate days, we arrive at the South Pole. We had done it.

Part 2

For the last eleven years, we have taken over 1,000 people, people from industry and business, women and men from companies, students from all over the world, down to Antarctica, and during those missions, we've managed to pull out over 1,500 tonnes of twisted metal left in Antarctica. That took eight years, and I'm so proud of it because we recycled all of it back here in South America.

[. . .] We have taken young people from industry and business from India, from China. These are game-changing nations, and will be hugely important in the decision about the preservation of the Antarctic.

[. . .] It is such a privilege to go to Antarctica, I can't tell you. I feel so lucky, and I've been 35 times in my life, and all those people who come with us return home as great champions, not only for Antarctica, but for local issues back in their own nations.

Part 3

NASA informed us six months ago that the Western Antarctic Ice Shelf is now disintegrating. Huge areas of ice – look how big Antarctica is even compared to here – huge areas of ice are breaking off from Antarctica, the size of small nations. And NASA have calculated that the sea level will rise, it is definite, by one metre in the next 100 years, the same time that my mum has been on planet Earth. It's going to happen, and I've realized that the preservation of Antarctica and our survival here on Earth are linked. And there is a very simple solution. If we are using more renewable energy in the real world, if we are being more efficient with the energy here, running our energy mix in a cleaner way, there will be no financial reason to go and exploit Antarctica. It won't make financial sense, and if we manage our energy better, we also may be able to slow down, maybe even stop, this great ice melt that threatens us.

[. . .] Antarctica is a moral line in the snow, and on one side of that line we should fight, fight hard for this one beautiful, pristine place left alone on Earth. I know it's possible. We are going to do it. And I'll leave you with these words from Goethe. I've tried to live by them.

'If you can do, or dream you can, begin it now, for boldness has genius, power and magic in it.'

Good luck to you all. Thank you very much.

Unit 10 Theaster Gates: How to revive a neighbourhood: with imagination, beauty and art

Part 1

The neighbourhood that I live in is Grand Crossing. It's a neighbourhood that has seen better days. It is not a gated community by far. There is lots of abandonment in my neighbourhood, and while I was kind of busy making pots and busy making art and having a good art career, there was all of this stuff that was happening just outside my studio.

[. . .] But I think a lot of our US cities and beyond have the challenge of blight – abandoned buildings that people no longer know what to do anything with. And so I thought, is there a way that I could start to think about these buildings as an extension or an expansion of my artistic practice? And that if I was thinking along with other creatives – architects, engineers, real estate finance people – that us together might be able to kind of think in more complicated ways about the reshaping of cities.

Part 2

And so I bought a building. The building was really affordable. We tricked it out. We made it as beautiful as we could to try to just get some activity happening on my block. Once I bought the building for about $18,000, I didn't have any money left. So I started sweeping the building as a kind of performance. This is performance art, and people would come over, and I would start sweeping. Because the broom was free and sweeping was free. It worked out. [Laughter] But we would use the building, then, to stage exhibitions, small dinners, and we found that that building on my block, Dorchester – we now referred to the block as Dorchester Projects – that in a way that building became a kind of gathering site for lots of different kinds of activity.

[. . .] One house turned into a few houses, and we always tried to suggest that not only is creating a beautiful vessel important, but the contents of what happens in those buildings is also very important. So we were not only thinking about development, but we were thinking about the programme, thinking about the kind of connections that could happen between one house and another, between one neighbour and another.

Part 3

In this bank that we called the Arts Bank, it was in pretty bad shape. There was about six feet of standing water. It was a difficult project to finance, because banks weren't interested in the neighbourhood because people weren't interested in the neighbourhood because nothing had happened there. It was dirt. It was nothing. It was nowhere. And so we just started imagining, what else could happen in this building?

And so now that the rumour of my block has spread, and lots of people are starting to visit, we've found that the bank can now be a centre for exhibition, archives, music performance, and that there are people who are now interested in being adjacent to those buildings because we brought some heat, that we kind of made a fire.

[. . .] In some ways, it feels very much like I'm a potter, that we tackle the things that are at our wheel, we try with the skill that we have to think about this next bowl that I want to make. And it went from a bowl to a singular house to a block to a neighbourhood to a cultural district to thinking about the city, and at every point, there were things that I didn't know that I had to learn.

[. . .] So now, we're starting to give advice around the country on how to start with what you got, how to start with the things that are in front of you, how to make something out of nothing, how to reshape your world at a wheel or at your block or at the scale of the city.

Thank you so much.

Unit 11 Erik Johansson: Impossible photography

Part 1

I'm here to share my photography. Or is it photography? Because, of course, this is a photograph that you can't take with your camera.

Yet, my interest in photography started as I got my first digital camera at the age of fifteen. It mixed with my earlier passion for drawing, but it was a bit different because using the camera, the process was in the planning instead. And when you take a photograph with a camera, the process ends when you press the trigger. So to me it felt like photography was more about being at the right place at the right time. I felt like anyone could do that.

So I wanted to create something different, something where the process starts when you press the trigger. Photos like this: construction going on along a busy road. But it has an unexpected twist. And despite that, it retains a level of realism. Or photos like these – both dark and colourful, but all with a common goal of retaining the level of realism.

Part 2

But what's the trick that makes it look realistic? Is it something about the details or the colours? Is it something about the light? What creates the illusion?

[. . .] I would like to say that there are three simple rules to follow to achieve a realistic result. As you can see, these images aren't really special. But combined, they can create something like this.

So the first rule is that photos combined should have the same perspective. Secondly, photos combined should have the same type of light. And these two images both fulfill these two requirements – shot at the same height and in the same type of light. The third one is about making it impossible to distinguish where the different images begin and end by making it seamless. Make it impossible to say how the image actually was composed.

Part 3

So to achieve a realistic result, I think it comes down to planning. It always starts with a sketch, an idea. Then it's about combining the different photographs. And here every piece is very well planned. And if you do a good job capturing the photos, the result can be quite beautiful and also quite realistic. So all the tools are out there, and the only thing that limits us is our imagination.

Thank you.

Unit 12 Myriam Sidibe: The simple power of handwashing

Part 1

So imagine that a plane is about to crash with 250 children and babies, and if you knew how to stop that, would you?

Now imagine that 60 planes full of babies under five crash every single day. That's the number of kids that never make it to their fifth birthday: 6.6 million children never make it to their fifth birthday.

Most of these deaths are preventable, and that doesn't just make me sad, it makes me angry, and it makes me determined. Diarrhoea and pneumonia are among the top two killers of children under five, and what we can do to prevent these diseases isn't some smart new technological innovations. It's one of the world's oldest inventions: a bar of soap.

[. . .] Handwashing with soap is one of the most cost-effective ways of saving children's lives. It can save over 600,000 children every year. That's the equivalent of stopping ten jumbo jets full of babies and children from crashing every single day.

Part 2

So now just take a minute. I think you need to get to know the person next to you. Why don't you just shake their hands? Please shake their hands. All right, get to know each other. They look really pretty. All right. So what if I told you that the person whose hands you just shook actually didn't wash their hands when they were coming out of the toilet? They don't look so pretty anymore, right? Pretty yucky, you would agree with me.

Well, statistics are actually showing that four people out of five don't wash their hands when they come out of the toilet, globally. And the same way we don't do it when we've got fancy toilets, running water and soap available, it's the same thing in the countries where child mortality is really high.

[. . .] So why is it? Why aren't people washing their hands? Why is it that Mayank, this young boy that I met in India, isn't washing his hands? Well, in Mayank's family, soap is used for bathing, soap is used for laundry, soap is used for washing dishes. His parents think sometimes it's a precious commodity, so they'll keep it in a cupboard. They'll keep it away from him so he doesn't waste it. On average, in Mayank's family, they will use soap for washing hands once a day at the very best, and sometimes even once a week for washing hands with soap. What's the result of that? Children pick up disease in the place that's supposed to love them and protect them the most, in their homes.

Part 3

Nine years ago, I decided, with a successful public health career in the making, that I could make the biggest impact coming, selling and promoting the world's best invention in public health: soap. We run today the world's largest handwashing programme by any public health standards. We've reached over 183 million people in 16 countries. My team and I have the ambition to reach one billion by 2020.

[. . .] Last week, my team and I spent time visiting mothers that have all experienced the same thing: the death of a newborn. I'm a mum. I can't imagine anything more powerful and more painful. This one is from Myanmar. She had the most beautiful smile, the smile, I think, that life gives you when you've had a second chance. Her son, Myo, is her second one. She had a daughter who passed away at three weeks, and we know that the majority of children that actually die, die in the first month of their life, and we know that if we give a bar of soap to every skilled birth attendant, and that if soap is used before touching the babies, we can reduce and make a change in terms of those numbers.

[. . .] I hope you will join us and make handwashing part of your daily lives and our daily lives and help more children like Myo reach their fifth birthday.

Thank you.

Irregular verb list

Infinitive	Past simple	Past participle	Translation	Infinitive	Past simple	Past participle	Translation
be	was / were	been		leave	left	left	
beat	beat	beaten		lend	lent	lent	
become	became	become		let	let	let	
begin	began	begun		lie	lay	lain	
bend	bent	bent		light	lit	lit	
bite	bit	bitten		lose	lost	lost	
blow	blew	blown		make	made	made	
break	broke	broken		mean /miːn/	meant /ment/	meant /ment/	
bring	brought	brought		meet	met	met	
build	built	built		must	had to	had to	
burn	burnt / burned	burnt / burned		pay	paid	paid	
burst	burst	burst		put	put	put	
can	could	been able to		read /riːd/	read /red/	read /red/	
catch	caught	caught		ride	rode	ridden	
choose	chose	chosen		ring	rang	rung	
come	came	come		rise	rose	risen	
cost	cost	cost		run	ran	run	
cut	cut	cut		sell	sold	sold	
do	did	done		send	sent	sent	
draw	drew	drawn		set	set	set	
drive	drove	driven		shake	shook	shaken	
eat	ate	eaten		shine	shone	shone	
fall	fell	fallen		show	showed	shown	
feed	fed	fed		shut	shut	shut	
feel	felt	felt		sing	sang	sung	
fight	fought	fought		sink	sank	sunk	
find	found	found		sit	sat	sat	
fly	flew	flown		sleep	slept	slept	
forget	forgot	forgotten		spell	spelt / spelled	spelt / spelled	
forgive	forgave	forgiven		spend	spent	spent	
freeze	froze	frozen		stand	stood	stood	
give	gave	given		steal	stole	stolen	
go	went	gone		stick	stuck	stuck	
grow	grew	grown		swear	swore	sworn	
have	had	had		swim	swam	swum	
hear /ˈhɪə/	heard /hɜːd/	heard /hɜːd/		take	took	taken	
hide	hid	hidden		teach	taught	taught	
hit	hit	hit		tear	tore	torn	
hold	held	held		think	thought	thought	
hurt	hurt	hurt		throw	threw	thrown	
keep	kept	kept		understand	understood	understood	
know	knew	known		wake	woke	woken	
lay	laid	laid		wear	wore	worn	
lead	led	led		win	won	won	

Keynote Elementary
Student's Book
David Bohlke
Stephanie Parker

Publisher: Gavin McLean

Publishing Consultant: Karen Spiller

Development Editor: Sarah Ratcliff

Editorial Manager: Claire Merchant

Head of Strategic Marketing ELT: Charlotte Ellis

Media Researcher: Leila Hishmeh

Senior Content Project Manager: Nick Ventullo

Manufacturing Manager: Eyvett Davis

Cover/Text Design: Brenda Carmichael

Compositor: MPS North America LLC

Audio: Tom Dick and Debbie Productions Ltd

DVD: Tom Dick and Debbie Productions Ltd

Cover Photo Caption: Flying machines demo by
Raffaello D'Andrea at TED2016 - Dream, February 15–19,
2016, Vancouver Convention Center, Vancouver, Canada.
Photo: © Bret Hartman/Ryan Lash/TED.

For product information and technology assistance, contact us at
Cengage Learning Customer & Sales Support, 1-800-354-9706

For permission to use material from this text or product, submit all
requests online at **cengage.com/permissions**

Further permissions questions can be emailed to
permissionrequest@cengage.com

Student's Book ISBN: 978-1-337-27391-6

National Geographic Learning
Cheriton House, North Way, Andover, Hampshire, SP10 5BE
United Kingdom

Cengage Learning is a leading provider of customized learning solutions
with employees residing in nearly 40 different countries and sales in more
than 125 countries around the world. Find your local representative at
www.cengage.com.

Cengage Learning products are represented in Canada by Nelson Education Ltd.

Visit National Geographic Learning online at **ngl.cengage.com**
Visit our corporate website at **www.cengage.com**

CREDITS

The publishers would like to thank TED Staff for their insightful feedback and expert guidance, allowing us to achieve our dual aims of maintaining the integrity of these inspirational TED Talks, while maximising their potential for teaching English.

The author and publisher would like to thank the following teaching professionals for their valuable input during the development of this series:

Coleeta Paradise Abdullah, Certified Training Center; Tara Amelia Arntsen, Northern State University; Estela Campos; Federica Castro, Pontificia Universidad Católica Madre y Maestra; Amy Cook, Bowling Green State University; Carrie Cheng, School of Continuing and Professional Studies, the University of Hong Kong; Mei-ho Chiu, Soochow University; Anthony Sean D'Amico, SDH Institute; Wilder Yesid Escobar Almeciga, Universidad El Bosque; Rosa E. Vasquez Fernandez, English for International Communication; Touria Ghaffari, The Beekman School; Rosario Giraldez, Alianza Cultural Uruguay Estados Unidos; William Haselton, NC State University; Yu Huichun, Macau University of Science and Technology; Michelle Kim, TOPIA Education; Jay Klaphake, Kyoto University of Foreign Studies; Kazuteru Kuramoto, Keio Senior High School; Michael McCollister, Feng Chia University; Jennifer Meldrum, EC English Language Centers; Holly Milkowart, Johnson County Community College; Nicholas Millward, Australian Centre for Education; Stella Maris Palavecino, Buenos Aires English House; Youngsun Park, YBM; Adam Parmentier, Mingdao High School; Jennie Popp, Universidad Andrés Bello; Terri Rapoport, ELS Educational Services; Erich Rose, Auburn University; Yoko Sakurai, Aichi University; Mark D. Sheehan, Hannan University; DongJin Shin, Hankuk University of Foreign Studies; Shizuka Tabara, Kobe University; Jeffrey Taschner, AUA Language Center; Hadrien Tournier, Berlitz Corporation; Rosa Vasquez, JFK Institute; Jindarat De Vleeschauwer, Chiang Mai University; Tamami Wada, Chubu University; Colin Walker, Myongii University; Elizabeth Yoon, Hanyang University; Keiko Yoshida, Konan University

And special thanks to: Craig Albrightson, Sam Cossman and Matt Caltabiano, Ross Donihue and Marty Schnure, Philip Jones, Mary Kadera, Bonnie Kim, Scott Leefe, Richard Lenton, David Matijasevich, Hannah Reyes

Although every effort has been made to contact copyright holders before publication, this has not always been possible. If contacted, the publisher will undertake to rectify any errors or omissions at the earliest opportunity.

The publishers would like to thank the following for permission to use copyright material:

Cover: © Bret Hartman/Ryan Lash/TED.

Photos: 6 (tl, bl) © James Duncan Davidson/TED; 6 (tr) © Michael Brands/TED; 6 (ml, br) © Bret Hartman/TED; 6 (mr) © TED; 7 (tl) © James Duncan Davidson/TED; 7 (tr, ml, br) © Ryan Lash/TED; 7 (mr) © Bret Hartman/TED; 7 (bl) © Robert Leslie/TED; 8 © Michael Brands/TED; 9 (t) © Solent News/REX/Shutterstock; 9 (b) © Amy Harris; 10 © Glenn Oakley; 11 © Tony Gribben; 13 © William Thoren; 14 © Joseph Llanes/Getty Images; 16 © James Duncan Davidson/TED; 17 © Karl Walter/Getty Images; 18 © Steve Debenport/Getty Images; 19 (t) © AP Photo/The Register-Guard, Brian Davies/AP Images; 19 (b) © Michael Brands/TED; 20 © Richard Nowitz/National Geographic Creative; 21 © GaudiLab/Shutterstock.com; 23 © Pedro Armestre/AFP/Getty Images; 24 © Stefano Amantini/Atlantide Phototravel; 26 © Michael Brands/TED; 27 © TED; 28 © mubus7/Shutterstock.com; 29 (t) © Peter Macdiarmid/Stringer/Getty Images; 29 (b) © Bret Hartman/TED; 30 © Robert Pratta/Reuters; 31 © Richard Lenton; 33 © Tiksa Negeri/Reuters; 34 © Hiroyuki Ito/Getty Images; 36 © Chris Burkard/Massif; 37 © Chris Burkard/Massif; 38 © Photobac/Shutterstock.com; 39 © Christopher Street; 41 (t) © Gary Friedman/Los Angeles Times/Getty Images; 41 (b) © TED; 42 © Essdras M Suarez/The Boston Globe/Getty Images; 43 © National Geographic Channel; 45 © epa european pressphoto agency b.v./Alamy Stock Photo; 46 © SeongJoon Cho/Bloomberg/Getty Images; 48 © TED; 49 © Guillem Lopez/Starstock/Photoshot/Newscom; 50 © William Taufic/Getty Images; 51 (t) © Matthew Mahon/Redux Pictures; 51 (b) © James Duncan Davidson/TED; 52 © jbor/Shutterstock.com; 53 © Sam Cossman/Barcroft Media/Getty Images; 55 © PRNewsFoto/Arx Pax/AP Images; 56 © WENN Ltd/Alamy Stock Photo; 58 (t) © Christophe Vollmer/Reuters; 58 (b) © Unimedia Europe/Unimediaimages Inc/Unimedia Europe/Newscom; 59 © WENN Ltd/Alamy Stock Photo; 60 © Westend61/

Printed in Greece by Bakis SA

Print Number: 01   Print Year: 2017